A Casebook
in Time-Limited
Psychotherapy

A Casebook in Time-Limited Psychotherapy

James Mann, M.D.

Robert Goldman, M.D.

JASON ARONSON INC.
Northvale, New Jersey
London

THE MASTER WORK SERIES

First softcover edition 1994

ISBN: 1-56821-210-0
Library of Congress Catalog Card Number: 93-74812

Manufactured in the United States of America. Jason Aronson Inc. offers books and cassettes. For information and catalog write to Jason Aronson Inc., 230 Livingston Street, Northvale, New Jersey 07647.

Dedicated to our wives and children

Contents

I could criticize this.

Preface

In the years that have passed since the publication of *Time Limited Psychotherapy*,[1] I have responded to invitations to lecture and to present workshops on the subject at a wide variety of public and private institutions and agencies in different parts of our country. University departments of psychiatry, university health services, private psychiatric hospitals, social work organizations and agencies, and others have listened, observed videotapes of actual treatment sessions, and raised questions. Some questions required amplification or further clarification of the treatment model and process. Others raised new issues, answers to which I sought through further study.

Eventually, it became apparent that no more really new questions were being raised. At that point, I thought it would be appropriate and useful to write another book, which would serve at least two major purposes. First, it would serve to share refinements in theory and technique, refinements brought to light not only through the many presentations but also through my continuing work with patients. Second, it would provide in-depth case material to demonstrate those refinements, as well as the range of treatable cases and the variety of outcomes. One case is presented in particularly extensive detail to illustrate the effectiveness of our method of selecting a central issue in overcoming racial

[1] James Mann, *Time Limited Psychotherapy*, Harvard University Press, Cambridge, Mass., 1973.

and socioeconomic-educational barriers. In the chapters that follow, the treatment in all cases described conforms to the Mann model presented in *Time Limited Psychotherapy,* a model that is distinctively different from other varieties of brief psychotherapy.

I am grateful to the many and varied audiences who listened, raised questions, and made me think further about the nature of the work. During the academic year 1975–1976, I conducted a tutorial in time-limited psychotherapy at the Boston Psychoanalytic Institute for both candidates in training and graduate analysts. In the course of the tutorial, two of the members treated patients and presented their material for group discussion. I am grateful to everyone in that group for the thoughtful questions and comments that their particular training and expertise provoked.

Of all my colleagues in Boston, the one who has shared with me the widest experience in time-limited psychotherapy is Robert Goldman. Our many discussions on various points of theory, process, and technique led naturally to our collaborative efforts in this volume.

Finally, a note of appreciation to my wife, Ida Mann, who is a senior social worker and student supervisor at the Jewish Family and Children's Service of Boston. Our discussions of her work with time-limited psychotherapy—both in treating clients and in teaching and training social workers—have added useful information on yet another kind of patient population.

I wish also to express my thanks to the Commonwealth Fund for a small grant that provided secretarial assistance.

James Mann

Acknowledgments

James Mann originated time-limited psychotherapy when he was Director of Residency Training in the Division of Psychiatry at the Boston University School of Medicine; Robert Goldman was a student in the same program. From its inception, time-limited psychotherapy was recognized by residents and faculty as both a powerful clinical and a unique training tool, in that it allowed residents both to observe rapid clinical improvement and to study transference and termination in a way not often possible in longer-term therapies, especially those conducted in the context of a training program. Time-limited psychotherapy has been employed in the training program with considerable success, and has been adopted by other institutions that have joined the Boston University family.

Over the years the authors have had many stimulating discussions on the theoretical and clinical aspects of time-limited psychotherapy, discussions that eventually led to collaboration on this book. We with to thank the many residents and faculty members of the Division of Psychiatry at Boston University School of Medicine whose efforts and comments have helped in the development of this work. Special thanks are extended to Drs. Sanford Cohen, Peter Knapp, and Stanley Cheren. The latter two read the manuscript and offered many helpful suggestions.

James Mann, M.D.
Robert Goldman, M.D.

When memory comes, knowledge comes too, little by little. Knowledge and memory are one and the same thing.

Saul Friedlander
When Memory Comes

1

A Review of the
Treatment Model

In this chapter, a review of the treatment structure and process will serve to introduce revisions and additions to the theory of time-limited psychotherapy. Some of what follows was detailed in *Time-Limited Psychotherapy.*[1] Additional information, gained from further experience in practice and through many discussions with colleagues, will illuminate parts of the earlier publication.

Long-term psychotherapy and psychoanalysis are assumed to be of indefinite duration. At best, patient and therapist have only a rough idea as to the probable duration of treatment—from two to five or more years. The patient (and perhaps the therapist as well) experiences the treatment as timeless; neither patient nor therapist tends to pay attention to the matter of time. In these modalities, time becomes a lively dynamic of the treatment process only when the question of termination is broached; or in connection with difficulty in paying for treatment, impending vacations of the therapist, a contemplated move by the patient to another city, or as a resistance to treatment. For practical purposes, in long-term psychotherapy or psychoanalysis, patients' only reactions to the conscious and

[1] James Mann, *Time Limited Psychotherapy,* Harvard University Press, Cambridge, Mass., 1973.

unconscious meaning and experience of time may be found in their unconscious fantasies in respect to the magical fulfillment of early, long wished-for needs. The indefinite length of the treatment is enough to create the feeling that the engagement is timeless.

All short forms of psychotherapy, whatever they are called, implicitly propose a time limit. Informing the patient that therapy will be brief or short-term is in itself enough to suggest a limit: the words "brief" and "short" have just that connotation. The patient may sometimes be told the projected number of sessions, subject, of course, to the progress of treatment. The uniqueness of time-limited psychotherapy, beyond the specific limitation of treatment to twelve sessions, lies in the fact that the time limit directly influences the progress and process of treatment, because of the unconscious meaning and experience of time in the course of personality development and because of its enduring role in giving meaning to the past, present, and future *affective* life of each person. Other short-term psychotherapies simply pay no attention to the implicitly stated role of time.

Recently, Malan,[2] a leading investigator and practitioner of brief psychotherapy, recognized this pointed omission; he now tells the patient at the start of treatment the precise date of termination. He thus recognizes the importance of dealing with termination in brief therapy. It does not appear, however, that he appreciates the ongoing dynamic significance of this kind of time limit in the total process of treatment.

Two kinds of time—categorical time and existential time—are generally recognized. The first is the time that we respond to in terms of the clock and calendar; the second is time that is experienced, *lived in.* The capacity to recognize and understand categorical time is intimately involved in the growing child's development of reality sense. Accompanying this development is the awareness that time is limited. Categorical time is real time, *adult time;* it makes one appreciate that there is an ultimate end to time—that is, death. In early childhood, before the recognition of categorical time, time is eternal, endless, *child time.*

Thus, in order to undo time sense, reality must be undone; and to undo reality, time sense must be undone. In the psychoses, the undoing of reality includes either a total loss of categorical time sense or an alteration in its boundaries, depending on the severity of the psychotic reaction. Prisoners in isolation for long periods of time preserve reality by devising methods of keeping tabs on the passage of real time. Our current life consists of memories of things past and expectations of the future; it is a fusion of eternal *child time* and finite *adult time.* Thus, we are caught in a

[2] David M. Malan, *The Frontier of Brief Psychotherapy,* Plenum, New York, 1976.

never-ending conflict between the reality of death and our denial of it, our expectation of immortality.[3]

We use time to integrate what was, what is, and what will be insofar as these relate to us personally. Historical events are interesting to most people, important to some, and decisive to still others. They are decisive to those whose concept of what was, what is, and what will be may be drastically altered by the event. To lose a loved one in war; to suffer the disintegration of a family during the depression of the thirties; to lose one's family in the Nazi holocaust; or, in a much smaller arena, to experience the loss of a loved one on the 4th of July or on Thanksgiving or Christmas—in all these examples, time is the decisive link between an objective, real experience and the internal or intrapsychic concept of the same episode. In other words, events of significance to us become memories, and memories always speak to the recollection (whether or not distorted) of events that are intimately related (often unconsciously) to important persons in our lives.

The memories may, in fact, turn out to be fantasies or retrospective falsifications in respect to time. We have all had patients who, early in treatment, were absolutely certain about the time and particulars of an important early event, only to find that it had occurred much later and in quite a different way than they had believed. Obviously, we cannot separate memories from time. It may be useful to note here that a good psychiatric interview, whether for history-taking or as a therapeutic session, serves to link events in time. As we review and pick up threads of the patient's past, present, and future, we help the patient to recognize the persistence with which time past, present, and future is experienced in repetitive feelings and behavior.

Melges[4] points out that "the basic components of psychological time consist of subjective tempo, sequence, and temporal perspective. These components are interrelated. Short intervals between sequences give rise to a fast subjective tempo and the inner tempo and rate may accelerate further when a task has to be accomplished within a limited future time span." He adds that there may be no awareness that time is passing if there is no pressing goal to be accomplished. Appelbaum[5] describes the operation of Parkinson's Law in psychotherapy: patients "shrink [the] time necessary to perform a task when little time is available, or expand

---

[3] E. Becker, *The Denial of Death,* Free Press, New York, 1973.

[4] F. T. Melges, personal communication.

[5] S. A. Appelbaum, "Parkinson's Law in Psychotherapy," *International Journal of Psychoanalytic Psychotherapy,* vol. 4, 1975, p. 427.

[it] when more time is available." This experience is familiar to us in the context of work deadlines.

Loewald[6] reminds us of the significant temporal phenomena and concepts of psychoanalysis, which are equally pertinent to dynamic psychotherapy or any therapy that pays attention to the functions of the mind. They are: remembering (memory), forgetting, regression, repetition, and anticipation. He notes the influence of the past on present thoughts, feelings, and behavior; the delay of gratification and action, sleep-wakefulness, and abnormalities in the subjective sense of elapsed time. Note, for example, how quickly or slowly therapy hours seem to pass with different patients.

The timelessness of the id is often mentioned, and sometimes misconstrued to mean that nothing in the id ever changes. Actually, the timelessness lies in its ceaseless demands for certain infantile gratifications without any apparent recognition that what once was no longer is. The phenomena of transference repeatedly display thoughts, feelings, and behavior which speak now to the past, now to the present, now to the future—and sometimes to all three at once. The latter occurrence should not be surprising since there is no such thing as a fixed moment in time. The experience of time is a reciprocal relationship: one cannot even think about one time mode without considering the other as well. In ordinary circumstances, they continually modify each other.

Any kind of psychological treatment is part of the experience of time insofar as the patient works toward facing up to his past so that he can gain some mastery over the present and be freer in shaping his future. The attempts to escape the constraints of time are familiar to us. In difficult moments some of us seek refuge in sleep; we flee demands on our time periodically by going off on holidays; we slow up the sense of pressure (and of time) with the predinner cocktail. The passage of time is commonly slowed by the use of marijuana. Antianxiety medication induces a sense of relaxation and the feeling that time is less pressing. Meditation, with its use of a repetitive, rhythmic, monotonous stimulus, aims at reducing awareness of the outside world and the passage of time. Often the subject is instructed not to glance at his or her watch during meditation.

We can identify two extremes of time experience. One is the experience of eternity; time seems to be suspended. Such suspensions are said to occur in mystic states, in states of ecstasy, under the influence of drugs, and in emotional states of exceptional intensity. The other extreme is the experience of fragmentation. One's world is experienced in bits and

---

[6] Hans W. Loewald, "The Experience of Time," *Psychoanalytic Study of the Child,* vol. 27, 1973.

pieces, none of which has meaning. Connections and relatedness between past, present, and future are broken so that each instant of time is empty and without meaning. We see this fragmentation in states of depersonalization and derealization as well as in acute psychotic decompensation.

Hartocollis[7] has paid particular attention to the relationship between time and affects. He states that the way a person assesses the value of his ongoing lived time is determined not by his awareness of external reality but by how he perceives his own state of adequacy in the face of some negative or challenging reality. The reality confronting the person may be internal or external. The ego perceives an important threat or challenge to its well-being and then assesses its capacity to cope with that threat or challenge. The ego's assessment is likely to be made on the basis of past experience, and if the conclusion it comes to is one of inadequacy, a painful state of tension arises, experienced as a loss of self-esteem, as helplessness, or as a narcissistic wound. Whether this tension within the ego emerges as anxiety or depression will be determined by the ego's orientation in time; that is, by the assessment of its state of adequacy as potential (having a future) or actual (past).

Gifford[8] writes that the emergence of an organized ego structure and the acquisition of time sense come about "as the infant learns to adapt his sleep-wakefulness pattern to the diurnal periodicity of maternal attention to his needs. This early adaptation to the outer world is transmitted to the infant as a function of time."

All considerations on the nature and vicissitudes of time sense turn to its inevitable connection with early object relations. From this developmental point of view, the intermingling of the sense of time and the genesis of affects points to the experience of time as always being accompanied by affect. An extreme example is the obsessive-compulsive character whose life is dictated by the clock, so to speak, and whose intolerance of this kind of servitude forces isolation of affects. As Melges has stated, "The various emotions link present circumstances with future outcomes in the light of an appraisal of past outcomes in similar situations."[9] Situations need not be factually similar; they may be entirely symbolically similar, giving rise to the same appraisal of one's adequacy. In ordinary circumstances, time remains a background presence. We are always aware of it, but it does not interfere with our ongoing experience. Time becomes oppressive when one suffers from a pathological state or

[7] P. Hartocollis, "Time as a Dimension of Affects," *Journal of the American Psychoanalytic Association,* vol. 20, no. 1, 1972.

[8] S. Gifford, "Sleep, Time and the Early Ego," *Journal of the American Psychoanalytic Association,* vol. 8, 1960, p. 26.

[9] F. T. Melges, personal communication.

faces an emergency. The greater the invasion of time into consciousness, the more likely is the presence of psychopathology. Depressed patients, for example, feel that everything worthwhile is in the past; for them there is no present or future. They thus feel immobilized—stuck in time. It may be that the sense of energy produced by antidepressants allows for the experience of gratification in the present.

The analytic experience of one of us (J.M.) revealed the presence of "golden memories." These are akin to screen memories: clearly defined, sharp-edged, streaming with bright, warm, golden sunlight, conveying a sense of great familiarity although they cannot consciously be placed in time or space. The analysis of such memories brings to light the representation of the early mother and the wish to be warmed, comforted, and nurtured by her forever. Jim Jones is reported to have cried "Mother, mother" during the horrible Jonestown mass suicide.

One's sense of time expands and contracts according to one's particular situation and feelings. In times of distress, time will seem to go on endlessly. Conversely, time speeds by in pleasurable situations. A child can barely contain his burning impatience to be a third-grader, or a sixth-grader, or a teenager, or old enough to gain his driving license. To young people, time moves very slowly. As we grow older and achieve meaningful milestones, time moves with increasing rapidity until we feel bedeviled by its swift passage. The recurrent return to modes and music of past decades bespeaks a nostalgic wish to halt the ever-increasing pace of time in a world whose technology has compressed previously long spans of time into brief moments. The differences between generations used to be measured over a decade or more. Now we measure it over a period of two to four years.

A clinical vignette illustrates the relationship between time and distance. A patient in analysis is involved in a tangled, rather chaotic love affair with a younger woman who decides to go off to a distant part of the world for several years. He mourns her loss, idealizes her, and remains preoccupied with her. Six months later, he receives a phone call from her and learns that she has been no more than forty miles away all this time. He now feels much less interested in her. Losing the woman had re-created old responses to loss, and he sought to hold on to her by idealizing her with fantasies of her remarkable achievements and experiences in the distant country. This idealization increased her value to him and intensified his longing for her. When she returned home—after revealing that she had never been far away—he valued her far less. The farther away the love object, the more distant she became in the patient's unconscious experience of time, and hence, the more closely she was related to the early, idealized, longed-for mother. The return of the love object brought back all the ambivalent feelings that had existed in his early relationship with his mother, and anger at separation and loss took over.

Homesickness offers another example of this phenomenon. Everything about home (mother) is idealized and painfully longed for. With the return home, the idealization is rapidly undone. Thus, the first day or two of a visit home is commonly experienced as a warm, wonderful reception; one feels like a valued guest. But often the next days are marked by disagreements, friction, and the return of all the old barriers created by ambivalence. The intensity of the ambivalent feelings is readily understood. The return home rekindles recollections of the distant past, of a time when one was freely nurtured and cared for by others. The temptation to return, to regress to that period, is countered by the wish to grow away from it, to be independent and apart. This battle is universal; it begins with the early separation-individuation process and is never totally resolved. This is the battle that is fought within the person who returns home; it is especially pronounced on national holidays when family gatherings are highlighted—for example, Thanksgiving and Christmas. The frictions and discords serve to conceal the true meaning of the underlying conflicting wishes. During World War II, soldiers overseas mused about mother, apple pie, and ice cream. The sweetness of all three had a very short life when the armies returned home.

A third example of the relationship between time and distance is seen in dreams in which persons or objects are very small, as if viewed through the wrong end of a telescope. Their diminutive size indicates their distance in space and time; they are figures from the remote past.

One does not *feel* the passage of time. We become aware of its passage indirectly when we observe the calendar or clock, when we are distressed, and when we suffer from the physical disabilities of aging. In the absence of ill health, a person has no sense of *feeling* old or growing older. The depressions of middle and old age invariably have among their precipitants some kind of physical change or disability that serves to remind one of the passage of time and of getting older. From this point of view, it is fair to say that any patient coming for help is in a state of distress and is therefore more aware than most of the passage of time. In addition, the older the patient, the more acute is that awareness.

Time is a source of confusion to us, and we express our ambivalence about it in many contradictory ways. Time is everything in our affective lives. Time is a great legalizer, a great teacher, a kind friend, a great leveler, a taskmaster, a liar, a sandpile, money. It is fleeting, out of joint, the only comforter. Father Time is portrayed as an old man with a beard and scythe, whereas immortality is portrayed as a woman. In the unconscious, one finds the origins of the fantasy of immortality in the return to the early mother—to child time.

On the clinical side, we can compare the patient's responses to offers of brief and long-term therapy. In both instances, the patient's uncertainty about whether he can be helped is enormously diminished when the therapist offers treatment. Consciously, the patient may continue to entertain doubts about his prospects; unconsciously, expectations of "cure" and magical fulfillment abound. Persons coming for relief of pain—whether physical, emotional, or both—unconsciously impute magical, omnipotent qualities to the helper. The unconscious fantasy often includes the wish and expectation that one will be totally transformed into the person one has always wished to be. This kind of magical thinking is a normal part of early personality development. Its persistence in the adult patient indicates an encompassing expectation that the therapist will, in effect, *turn back time*. This is true of any therapeutic modality: psychotherapy, psychoanalysis, psychopharmacology, and all of the behavior modification techniques. The adult in the patient appreciates the uncertainties of the situation, the fee he will have to pay, the length of each session, the work he will have to do, and the possible duration of treatment. The child in the patient expects that his magical thinking will now come true and he will be returned to that earlier period of his life when time was endless and the warmth and comfort of the mother made everything pleasurable. As a result, the greater the ambiguity about the duration of treatment, the greater the influence of child time on unconscious wishes and expectations. The greater the specificity about the duration of treatment, the sooner child time will be confronted with reality and the work to be done.

In his paper, "The Problem of Ego Identity," Erikson[10] speaks of the experience of time in delayed and prolonged adolescence, noting that "there is a sense of great urgency and yet also a loss of consideration for time as a dimension of living. The young person may feel simultaneously very young, and in fact baby-like, and old beyond rejuvenation." In time-limited psychotherapy, one cannot expect regression to the point where the patient becomes preoccupied and engrossed with thoughts and feelings of his earliest years. Infantile amnesia is best lifted in psychoanalysis, much less readily lifted in long-term psychotherapy, and not touched at all in short-term psychotherapy. In time-limited psychotherapy, however, the patient's adolescent experiences are often revived, and since adolescence is a time of great emotional plasticity, with the intrusion of all major earlier conflicts, the therapist may learn a great deal about the patient's earlier life even in the absence of regression to that period. In time-limited psychotherapy, too, the treatment plan arouses an optimistic sense of urgency tempered by a sense of pessimism and predetermined disappointment.

When the therapist has obtained from the patient a thorough enough

[10] E. Erikson, "The Problem of Ego Identity," *Journal of the American Psychoanalytic Association,* vol. 4, no. 1, January 1956, p. 26.

history to allow for the formulation of the central issue (see Chapter 2), he then offers the patient a treatment proposal. The patient is informed about the nature of his problem through the therapist's formulation of the central issue. The patient's acceptance of the formulation is followed by an explanation of the treatment proposal. The explanation includes the exact duration of each meeting, the frequency of meetings, and the date of the twelfth and final session. Once all the details have been proffered, one pays careful attention to securing the patient's agreement to the proposal. Some patients will hasten to agree lest the therapist change his mind. Others will ask questions first. A common question is whether twelve sessions will be sufficient; a suitable response would be that the therapist believes the work on the central issue can be done in that period of time. Others will ask whether the *therapist* thinks that twelve sessions are enough; here the therapist should respond with a quietly reassuring "Yes."

In this connection, the role of suggestion in this treatment method is frequently questioned. Suggestion plays an inevitable part in every conceivable method of psychological and physical treatment. The questions that a therapist raises, the kinds of clarifications and interpretations that he makes—all serve as clues and cues to what the therapist believes is important, and the patient frequently responds to what is perceived as a suggested direction. The beneficial effect of the therapist's enthusiasm for the medication he offers his patients is a well-documented phenomenon. The therapist's tone of voice, body posture, and general mood on a given day all become suggestive influences on the patient. There is something to be said for giving a distressed person a sense of hope, particularly when the therapist knows that he has no intention of telling the patient how to live his life and that the treatment will aim at helping the patient gain an appreciation of choices in respect to feelings about the self, as well as to behavioral possibilities that had not been available before. Finally, one may ask whether quietly reassuring the patient could have a disappointing, or even harmful, effect on treatment. None of the patients we have treated have become worse; some have been disappointed about the extent of change, but all have profited to a greater or lesser degree.

Still other questions that may arise can usually be understood as resistance stimulated by and directly related to the central issue. For example, the central issue as stated to the patient, though not explicitly directed to the patient's dependent needs, may clearly carry dependency as a major problem. The patient may then raise seemingly realistic questions or doubts about the efficacy of twelve sessions, which are actually only a disguise for the already recognized dependency issue.

To illustrate another kind of resistance, let us look at a depressed man in his late forties. He was told that the problem confronting him stemmed from the difficulty he had as an only son in fulfilling the expectations of his parents; that despite his successes, he has always felt second-rate, inferior, and rejected. The patient agreed to this statement but then revealed his need to disagree, resist, and otherwise obstruct the course of treatment, not because he did not wish to become well, but rather because he responded to the treatment proposal as the kind of expectation he had long ago learned to resent and fear. The therapist must also be alert to the patient who rushes to accept everything in the treatment plan in an attempt to please the therapist. The patient must be asked to think about what is offered and thus be given the opportunity to raise questions or express doubts.

The final acceptance of the treatment agreement in all its details sets off a series of dynamic events that have been stimulated by the explicit time limitation and the statement of the central issue, which, as will be seen, also encompasses the element of time.

In all varieties of psychotherapy, the patient knows when therapy has begun, but he is seldom fully aware of the middle of treatment and usually does not recognize the end of treatment until the subject is explicitly discussed. In time-limited psychotherapy, the beginning, middle, and end are known from the start. The adult in the patient cannot escape these realities; the child in the unconscious of the patient will choose not to accept reality and will respond to the time structure with the expectation of a return to the earliest past, where reparations for all inflicted pains will be made and where finite time does not exist. Thus, while the adult patient is aware of the brevity of twelve sessions, he also has the *feeling* that twelve sessions is a long time. This feeling is accentuated when the treatment is conducted on a once-a-week basis and hence extends over a period of approximately three months. That the work will be accomplished in twelve meetings creates a feeling of optimism, but it is accompanied by disappointment apparently related to the feeling that a good thing already has a known ending. Thus the treatment structure mobilizes all of the patient's contradictory feelings about time.

The first phase of treatment, extending over the first three or four sessions, tends to be characterized by two major occurrences. First, the great optimism nurtured by the patient's unconscious expectations tends to create a therapeutic relationship that is often remarkably unambivalent and positive. Second, there is considerable relief of accumulated tensions through the abreaction that takes place as the patient responds to the central issue by opening the gates of his feelings about all the injustices that have been, as he feels, inflicted on him. A rapid working alliance and positive transference appear and, in this setting, the presenting symptoms and complaints tend to disappear. A transference cure is effected as the patient affectively experiences the therapist as the early important figure in the patient's life.

In the second phase of treatment, roughly the middle four sessions, the patient displays a return of ambivalence about both the therapist and the possible outcome of treatment. Nothing magical has happened, and signs of disappointment in the therapist and in the therapy begin to appear. The therapist will be in error if he responds to these changes personally and does not recognize that the ambivalence he is witnessing is but a repetition of the ambivalence the patient experienced when disappointment, frustration, and anger made their appearance in the relationship with the earlier figure(s) in his life. The patient's history, along with elaborations obtained during the first phase, will have illuminated the critical early events that were sufficient reason for deep-seated distress in the relationship with the important earlier figure or figures. Rather than reducing the patient's disappointment, one should encourage it for further exploration. Some particularly evident signs of ambivalence during this phase of treatment are the return of symptoms or complaints, lateness or absence from sessions, and overt or covert expressions of negative feelings about the therapist.

Again, a suitable analogy for the middle phase of time-limited psychotherapy can be found in the well-known phenomena that occur when sons and daughters visit home on Thanksgiving and Christmas. Such times are notable for giving and receiving. Food, drink, and gifts highlight these holidays. The symbolic return to the endless, dependent days of childhood becomes very real for a brief time. Soon, however, the shadow of separation begins to intrude once more. To end the visit home is imperative; if we yield to the wish to prolong the visit indefinitely, we know that we will also have to yield our independence and autonomy. The impulse to regress to what was once a shelter from the world must be confronted.

In such a confrontation we see two parallel courses of feeling. One course consists of the revival of all the old feelings of injustice: the hurts inflicted by others and the extent to which one felt victimized—in short, feeling sorry for oneself. The other course of feeling is a surge of antagonism, irritation, and annoyance, along with a readiness for flare-ups in the face of relative trivialities. These feelings conceal the wish to be dependent. It is in the midst of these angry feelings that one decides that it is once more time to leave home. This kind of decision must be made on each visit, even when everyone knows the length of the visit is limited by the need to return to a job, to school, or the like.

The affective course of events described here is repeated during the middle phase of treatment. The shadow of separation intrudes once the midpoint of treatment has been reached. The child in the unconscious of the patient wishes to remain; the adult knows that he must go and that he wishes to go in order to best serve his own interests. The ambivalent dilemma emerges in the patient's discouragement, disappointment, and renewed symptoms or complaints.

The third, or termination, phase is crucial. Depending on the awareness of the patient, the work of termination will take place during the last three—or possibly four—sessions. During the termination phase the patient will seek to repeat his earliest separation from a meaningful person without resolving the ambivalence that began with that person. That is to say, he will automatically respond to the impending separation and loss with the same *affect* that characterized the earliest separation and loss as well as all subsequent ones. The separation will be heavily laden with anger, rage, sadness, guilt, fear, and inevitable associations to the past. The aim of the new separation is to achieve separation with a degree of resolution sufficient to allow for a new kind of internalization with less anger, sadness, guilt, and fear. The termination process, with its final elaboration of the central issue, contributes to the patient's differentiation of himself from the therapist as a transference figure and, by the same token, from figures of his past. This process will result in a greater sense of self, a stronger ego, and a changed superego that allows the patient to regard himself more charitably.

Psychological processes and individual differences cannot be stereotyped. For this reason the three stages described above may overlap. In some patients, the stages will be remarkably distinct; in others they may be vague. The termination phase, however, is clearly demarcated and visible to the therapist's observing eye and ear. In any case, an awareness of these phases, with particular attention to a clear midpoint and endpoint, will help the therapist to understand the patient, to conceptualize the process, and to plan his interventions.

In long-term psychotherapy and in psychoanalysis, the elaboration of the central issue is essentially a lengthy uncovering of its multiple sources, its genesis in the psychosocial and psychosexual stages of development, the defenses erected against it, and the adaptive means for coping with it. In time-limited psychotherapy, careful history-taking allows for the recognition of the central issue as a felt fact in the patient's life. The therapist's presentation of it fosters its recognition by the patient. The treatment plan and structure confine the exploration and resolution of the central issue to its two major *affective* sources, namely, *reunion* and *separation.* The issue is thus confined within the bounds and meaning of time, the beginning of time and the end of time, of eternity and of death, of fantasy (fiction) and of reality. The clarity of the central issue and its affective centrality, along with the maintenance of that issue and its derivatives, without diversion into so many other areas of the patient's emotional life, results in something precise, both cognitively and affectively, being learned and experienced about the self within a treatment structure that aims at that goal.

It is worth noting here that in follow-up interviews six to twelve months after the final meeting, patients display an impressive degree of recall of the details of the work done during the twelve sessions. Usually, the patient recalls the central issue either precisely or in a very good paraphrase. Even more notable is the extent to which the patient experiences the follow-up interview as a reunion, with its optimism and expectancy, the appearance of disappointment with ambivalence, and finally separation. This phenomenon in follow-up interviews illustrates an important dynamic consequence of the treatment process in time-limited psychotherapy. Early (childhood and adolescent) traumata, insults, and injustices cannot be undone, nor can the powerful affects arising from them be erased. What treatment makes possible is an increased conscious awareness of such traumata, the objects on which they have been focused, the concomitant fantasies about the self, and the accompanying affects. This awareness leads to a greater tolerance of unpleasurable feelings (anxiety, guilt, anger, shame), followed by a reduction in the immediate employment of *automatic* defense mechanisms. The automatic response is replaced by a more conscious selection of responses in accordance with present reality. A more rewarding, adaptive response follows. Changes in the ego's perception of the self are accompanied by less harsh superego demands, with a consequent lessening of guilt and increase in self-esteem.

For example, a 54-year-old woman (Mrs. R—See Chapter 9) experienced a most terrifying family situation, which was followed by unremitting distress as important members of her family blamed her for what had happened. One of her aims in coming for treatment was to be able to forget the ever-recurring remembrance of the event and its aftermath. In her follow-up interview, she remarked that she was no longer tortured by the recall; it was done with. She added that although she would never forget it, she was now able to forgive those involved. At the end of the interview, she remarked that this follow-up interview, too, had been of great help to her.

One more word about the follow-up interview. At no time during the treatment does the therapist make any mention of a follow-up interview. It is incumbent on the therapist to make certain that the separation phase of treatment is unequivocal; anything less will suggest to the patient that the separation is not genuine, that more time will be available. Follow-up is instituted by phone or letter, in terms of the therapist's wish to learn how the patient has been getting along since termination. During the follow-up interview, no mention should be made of any further such interviews.

We are often asked, Why are there precisely twelve sessions? Why not fourteen, or eighteen, or twenty-five? When this method of short-term psychotherapy was first formulated, the number twelve was chosen entirely on empirical grounds. It was thought that twelve sessions might offer the patient enough time to develop a working alliance, to elaborate and work through the important problem. Once a twelve-session therapy course was established, it became important to avoid deviations in order to gain substantial experience using only one schedule, so that over time a more reasonable estimate of the assets and liabilities of the method could be established. Important research on the nature, process, and outcome of psychotherapy is facilitated by fixing the same time limit for each case. In addition, one circumvents the problems created by the overwhelming amount of information that accrues in longer-term treatments.

Other time schedules might be used with this model. However, the inclination toward longer time schedules must be considered in the light of the therapist's inclination to believe that, given more time, more can be accomplished. Although in particular cases that may be true, in most instances there is little if any evidence that longer necessarily means better. The common pattern in psychotherapy of any kind is for patients to make gains early in treatment, only to have progress grind to a halt for long periods as the patient's resistance mounts as a result of conflicts over passive-dependent wishes, the wish not to grow up, the fear of losing the therapist if improvement ensues, and more. It has long been observed that many patients can use a "thirty-minute hour" as effectively as a sixty-minute hour. Constrictions of time, such as the use of "deadlines," tend to mobilize the patient's demands on himself to complete a piece of work.

That the demands are also experienced as coming from someone else should not be judged as unfair, rigid, or authoritarian. Even if it were possible for a therapist of any persuasion to be entirely free of his own expectations of a patient (and it is not possible), the patient would still feel that he had to perform for the therapist. Perhaps in cases of severe superego defects or narcissistic character disorders, where patients are incapable of perceiving others' expectations of them, the time limit would be experienced as unfair and unacceptable. In all other cases, it is important not to minimize, as an impetus to constructive work, what the patient thinks the therapist expects of him. The patient may react to the imposition of a time limit as an expression of the therapist's confidence in the patient's ability to change within a particular time span. The patient is then eager to have the chance to live up to an aspect of his unconscious ego ideal. (Parenthetically, it should be noted that the number twelve has some interesting meanings in respect to time and distance. The signs of the zodiac are twelve, there are twelve months in the year, and the clock is divided into two segments of twelve hours each.)

At this point it is appropriate to discuss criticisms that may arise among therapists who believe that holding so firmly to termination after twelve sessions is arbitrary, inconsiderate of the patient's needs or wishes, and contrary to the position that psychotherapy should always be negotiated fairly and equally between therapist and patient. Some may even believe that this kind of termination is sadistic. A common question is: How does the therapist know that enough work has been done? What if the patient appears to need more help?

First, it would be well to consider several situations that can be exceptions to termination at the twelfth session. One such situation would be a sudden, disruptive event during the termination phase: for example, the death of a close relative or even the significant early person dealt with in the course of treatment. Any unexpected personal catastrophe is apt to be sufficient reason for extending the course of treatment. The duration of the extension will depend on the patient's capacity to manage loss, his mode of adapting to loss, the relationship of the loss to the central issue, and the nature of the catastrophe itself. For instance, one patient, a university student, had lost his father when he was 5 years old and had suffered from chronic depression with intermittent suicidal thoughts. In the tenth session, the patient reported with great distress that a former roommate, who lived on the same dormitory floor, had just committed suicide. The therapist continued the termination phase for two additional meetings and concluded treatment in fourteen sessions with a very good result.

In another case, the patient called the therapist about two months after termination and asked to see him. Her request was immediately granted and it became apparent that further work needed to be done on the separation issue. This work was satisfactorily completed in two extra meetings.

There are important reasons why the treatment should be completed in the agreed-on twelve sessions. The nodal points of the treatment are reunion and separation. Pain, which was once real, has become a guiding fiction in the life of the patient. Fantasies about oneself must be replaced by appreciation of the present reality about oneself. The chronic hostile-dependent attachment to figures from the past must be diminished and relinquished. If the therapist fails to end the treatment at the agreed-on time because of his own objections, the following conclusions can be drawn. The therapist simply has not done the work he should have, usually because he has not permitted himself to work directly and without fear on his own inhibitions with respect to the separation-termination issue during the final two or three sessions. Yielding to one's anxieties about separation-termination and prolonging the treatment become a vote of no confidence in the patient. The adult patient, with rare exceptions, has strengths and assets that should not be underestimated. Prolonging the treatment reinforces the old hostile-dependent attachment and humiliates the adult in the patient. Sadism is more often visible in the therapist's clinging to the patient under the guise of serving the patient's projected needs, rather than giving the patient the dignity and freedom to take responsibility for finishing the work. The therapist must be keenly alert to his own separation problems in order to deal effectively with the patient's difficulties in separating from the therapist.

Clearly, the practice of time-limited psychotherapy calls for the active participation of the therapist. The rapidity with which the central issue and the time limitation move the patient into an active process demands that the therapist be ahead of the patient, that he understand where the patient is headed. Unlike longer-term psychotherapy, or in instances of brief psychotherapy in which the therapist leaves open the duration of the treatment, in time-limited psychotherapy one cannot sit back and expect important points that have been missed to turn up again at some later time. The therapist must respond promptly to the overt clues and subtle nuances provided by the patient. At the same time, the therapist must maintain an investigative, clarifying, and interpretive stance that allows the patient to move toward greater independence and a greater sense of self through his own efforts. To the extent that self-discipline and training allow, we refrain from telling the patient what to do and from imposing our own ideas or values, yet we engage the patient actively. There is room for much activity in the course of investigating, clarifying, and interpreting, and there is room for much passive listening when the patient is working effectively. Disciplined flexibility is essential.

Close attention to the central issue throughout the treatment not only becomes the guiding principle for the therapist but also serves to convey to the patient the humanness of the therapist. It is the patient's sense of self that is our concern, and it is how that distorted sense of self is played out with us that makes the therapist "real." There is no need for extravagant gestures of caring since a remarkable degree of caring is contained in the nature of the model and process alone.

It may be helpful to comment on some common termination situations in time-limited psychotherapy. In the eleventh and twelfth sessions, the patient may report that things are back to their previous awful state and asks the therapist what to do about it. Knowing all the work that has already been done on the central issue, the therapist's helpful response may be along the following lines: "From the work we have done together,

I know that you will be able to manage very well." The therapist, who is a very meaningful person to the patient, is expressing a vote of confidence in the patient's willingness and ability to grow and change.

In time-limited psychotherapy there is an impressive control of regression and minimal acting out. An important exception may be noted in the tenth or eleventh session, when the patient may engage in a piece of acting out which, fortunately, is rarely serious. It usually consists of behavior that is clearly motivated by angry feelings more properly directed to the therapist because of the impending separation. A patient may have a seemingly unprovoked outburst with a spouse or authority figure or may engage in some kind of minor self-punitive action. Whatever the action, it should be brought promptly into the treatment session for direct exploration and clarification of its meaning in the context of the transference.

The patient may ask what he should do if the pain (symptoms, complaints) returns at some future time. A helpful response would be, "You know enough about yourself to be able to deal with it in the way that you would like . . . moreover, be good to yourself, give yourself time to digest further what you and I have done here."

Finally, the patient may inquire what he should do if he really needs help again. The most helpful response is to tell the patient that he will know what to do. This may seem like a cryptic remark, but it is really a tribute to the adult in the patient, who will understand the remark to mean that he is capable of contacting the therapist if need be.

It is not possible to elaborate on every contingency. The common ones have been stated and, since human beings are distinguished by their uniqueness, new situations can always be anticipated. Understanding of the treatment structure and its theoretical underpinnings, as well as repeated experience and sharing with other therapists doing the same work, will reinforce one's confidence and effective management of patients in time-limited psychotherapy. The therapist will find that time-limited psychotherapy is an intensely *affective* experience for both patient and therapist. As long as he understands and adheres to the treatment model, the therapist will never be bored or find his attention drifting; rather, he will find himself exposed to a great deal of affect and will obtain much pertinent information in a short period of time. A dynamic process has been set in motion by design, and it is the therapist's responsibility to keep abreast of it so that he can help the patient.

Time-limited psychotherapy is not for the beginning therapist; the best preparation for it is extensive experience in long-term psychotherapy so that one can gain a full appreciation for the unconscious functions of the mind, the ego defenses, transference, and resistance. Experience has demonstrated that this model of time-limited psychotherapy is a valuable device for teaching supervisees to recognize very directly and clearly the meaning and power of transference and of the resistance to termination. Extensive reading on these issues is not particularly helpful, and the dilution of the process that so often occurs in long-term psychotherapy may further obscure them. Even after a personal analysis, which validates these issues most conclusively, the therapist still requires the help of experienced supervisors to translate his personal experience into a therapeutic tool. Peer supervision with experienced therapists is most useful for learning how to arrive at a meaningful central issue from the patient's history and for following the course of treatment to a successful conclusion. From such cooperative peer groups, there will then emerge a cadre of supervisors who can help the less experienced in doing the rewarding work of time-limited psychotherapy.

2

The Selection of the Central Issue

Time-limited psychotherapy exercises its influence through the two major points of the treatment proposal: the setting of the termination date at the start of treatment and the therapist's statement of the central issue, which describes the patient's major problem. The process that these points set in motion illuminates the relationship between persistent negative feelings about the self over time and the origins of these feelings arising out of the inability to effect separation without suffering damage to feelings about the self. We have already dealt with the unconscious meaning of time and its influence on treatment. Continuing experience has helped to refine both the method of selecting a central issue out of a considerable mass of data and its significance in facilitating the early appearance of a therapeutic or working alliance.

In all short forms of psychotherapy, attention must be directed very quickly to the question of which of the patient's problems is to be the center of the task in the brief time available. Generally the patient's presenting complaint, or what appears to be the most important of the patient's complaints, becomes the agreed-upon task. Such a selection is particularly appropriate in long-term psychotherapy, where the intent is to understand, analyze, and slowly dissolve the resistance maintained by various ego defenses. In any brief psychotherapy, and certainly in this mode of treatment where time is specifically limited, it is not at all feasible to work one's way through the layers of defense. In time-limited psychotherapy, the central issue as posed by the therapist must be one that, among other things, will bypass defenses, control the patient's anxiety, and stimulate the rapid appearance of a therapeutic or working alliance as well as a positive transference. With such therapy, a process must be set in motion very quickly.

In coming for help, patients present themselves, their complaints, and their "story." Complaints may center on a physical ailment or on specific symptoms, such as a phobia, depression, or anxiety. The strategy of interviewing lies in making it possible for the patient to elaborate on his symptoms or complaints, and this is done by eliciting his life story. The further intent is that the life story (including the detailed circumstances of the patient's present situation) will disclose developmental data, repetitive conflict situations, and the patient's usual mode of managing conflict, so that one can understand the presenting complaints in terms of the patient's emotional continuum. This kind of interviewing search is especially important when the patient's complaint centers on a vague dissatisfaction with his current status, a sense of unfulfillment, and the like. In any case, the complaints that bring the patient for help may be understood as a final common pathway which, in the course of its construction, has been subjected to various ego defenses in order to keep out of awareness the impulses and wishes that threaten to enter consciousness.

All neurotic complaints are expressions of unconscious conflict. Treatment must aim to uncover and expose that unconscious conflict in order to subject it to reality and the test of its appropriateness to the patient's *present* life situation, as opposed to the very different situation that gave rise to the conflict. How shall we achieve this aim when our time for treatment is brief? The answer to this question is that the therapist must choose a "central issue": that is, a major complaint or focus. In practice, one generally chooses what seems to be the patient's most important presenting complaint, which one can expect to be heavily buttressed by longstanding defenses. The limitations of time demand that one bypass the defensive wall without subjecting the patient to intolerable anxiety. Clinicians are familiar with the hazards of undoing defenses too rapidly.

In time-limited psychotherapy, a central issue can be posed that bypasses defenses, controls the patient's anxiety, and stimulates a rapid working alliance and positive transference. The effectiveness of this kind of central issue is intimately linked with the explicit limitation of time and the conscious and unconscious meaning of that kind of limitation for the patient. In the absence of change, there is no sense of past, present, or future. In our patients, rigidly held conceptions of the self have their parallel in the conviction that nothing about the self can change. A negative self-sameness persists even in the face of reality evidence to the contrary. The central issue that we formulate directs the patient's attention to this "fixation" and circumscribes the area of work for the twelve sessions.

Let us elaborate. In taking a medical history, one elicits data in order to detect those events in the patient's life that affect, or may affect, his physical well-being. Likewise, in the psychiatric interview, we seek to uncover difficult or traumatic events, overt and covert, that occurred in the patient's life. How did the patient respond to recurrent painful events in his life? Such recurrent events need not be wholly similar in fact; their symbolic similarity is enough to evoke the same response in the patient. We refer here to events and responses that *recur,* not to single, isolated events. An exception would be the experience of an overwhelmingly catastrophic event that no one could experience without damage, regardless of previous history and personality structure. Imprisonment in a Nazi concentration camp is such an event.

Since we are interested in recurrent events and responses, it follows that not everything a patient tells us is important. In psychotherapy much time is consumed seeking the significance of events that are, in fact, insignificant because they are isolated, nonrecurrent instances. They do not have an existence over time. The central issue must be linked with the patient's time line, or history, and the various affects attached to it. People who come for help are, by definition, troubled and in pain. They disguise the particular nature of their pain in words—and, to a certain extent, in feelings—that serve to describe their symptoms. The symptoms or complaints are a means of preventing awareness of the unconscious conflict and of avoiding even preconscious awareness of the nature of the pain.

Our method of selecting the central issue is to extract from the patient's history that privately felt, rarely verbalized, *present* and *chronically endured pain. The pain is an important statement about how one feels and has always felt about the self.* It is a private pain that one does not reveal to others, and it flits recurrently through the mind, only to be suppressed and promptly denied. The chronic pain is the affective component of the patient's belief that he has been victimized. In fact, it is difficult to discern any kind of neurotic or emotional conflict in which the patient does not feel himself to have been the unjust victim. Our patients are asking us to recognize that they have been unjustly treated.

As young children, all of us were "victims" of a sort, at the mercy of others because of our helplessness. In all too many instances, however, the patient has been severely and genuinely victimized. The childhood victimization tends to become perpetuated as a guiding fiction in the life of the adult. That is, the adult continues to respond to certain events as he did when he was a child. What was once real in the life of the child continues into adult life as a fiction about oneself; the sensitized adult inappropriately responds to events as if they were repetitions of childhood experiences.

For example, it is not uncommon to see patients of considerable accomplishment who, although aware that their accomplishments are fully recognized by others, carry within themselves a heavy sense of inadequacy and failure. The guiding fiction of the adult may appear in the same terms as the original insults; or the original insults may be turned on the self in order to defend against anger. Stated another way, in some instances the self feels the sense of injury directly while in others self-blame disguises and conceals the injury. The example noted above, the person of considerable accomplishment who feels the pain of inadequacy, illustrates the turning on the self.

All patients have a conscious and unconscious wish for redress of the grievances. It is conscious in that the patient wishes for appropriate recognition of his need by his contemporaries in his contemporary world. His contemporaries, of course, have no way of recognizing that need since they are regularly confronted with the person's coping devices, which effectively disguise his pain. Unconsciously, there is the wish for reunion with the early important person or persons because the patient believes that those he holds directly responsible for the pain would be the most desirable healers. In this connection, the time limit, with its induction of magical expectations, facilitates the hope that reunion with the original figures will be effected. The statement of the central issue in terms of the present and chronically endured pain is so unlike anything that the patient has previously encountered as recognition of his private statement about himself that it, too, serves to enhance the expectation that restitution will be made.

This expectation becomes visible in the first three or four sessions of the treatment, during which the patient devotes most of his time to an outpouring of the hurts he has suffered; he reveals an enormous mass of significant anamnestic material and experiences all the effects of abreaction. Abreaction is the discharge of pent-up feelings surrounding any particular event or number of events in the life of the patient. While offering brief emotional relief, abreaction does not cure anything; its usefulness lies in clearing away the underbrush, so to speak. That is, after discharging his pent-up feelings, the patient can look at himself somewhat more dispassionately and can thus begin to focus on his painful problem.

The present and chronically endured pain is preconscious. That is, in certain circumstances the affective situation promptly arouses awareness of the pain, which subsides equally promptly as it is submerged by repetitive coping efforts (e.g., the need to please). The therapist's statement of the pain is in the nature of a clarification that the patient readily recognizes. It is also readily felt and fixed in the patient's attention by the therapist's adherence to it in the course of treatment. The statement of the central issue in terms of the present and chronically endured pain reverberates from the deepest levels of the unconscious, through the layers of ego defenses, and in the patient's conscious experience of himself in the present. It spans the patient's experience of time from the remote past to the immediate present to the expectable future. It speaks to the exquisite poignancy with which each person privately experiences his being. *With few exceptions, therefore, the central issue as formulated by the therapist in time-limited psychotherapy will be very different from the problems that the patient states as his reasons for seeking help.*

The varieties of chronic and presently endured pain are limited by the finite range of feelings available to human beings. These feelings may be subsumed under a few major headings:

Glad

Sad

Mad

Frightened

Guilty

Any other feelings will be derivatives of or within the range of these five. For example:

Glad: loving, happy, contented, euphoric, peaceful, wanted

Sad: unhappy, discontented, depressed, unwanted

Mad: irritated, annoyed, angry, furious, raging, irked

Frightened: anxious, nervous

Guilty: troubled, uneasy, ashamed

Because the range of affects available to humankind is limited, the present and chronically endured pain can be identified in all patients, irrespective of education and socioeconomic status. Further, the pain is universal; it varies only in its expression in the unique life experiences of each person. Each life story is absolutely unique in the people involved and in the events that have occurred, but all are absolutely alike in the limited number of feelings experienced. As treatment continues, the universal pain quickly expands outward across time into the present and downward into the infinite time of the remote past.

The statement of the central issue in these terms directly links past, present, and future; that is, the patient's private time line and the affects that accompany memories, regressions, fantasies, developmental arrests, and spurts—all of which eventually emerge as the unspoken, painful self-image. It is this time-bound self-image that brings the patient to us for help. It is obscured by the host of complaints, symptoms, and character traits with which we are familiar. It should be noted that the kind of central issue we have described is not one the patient could reach by himself in the course of evaluation interviews, *nor does it speak to the patient's conflict with significant others*. Rather, it is saying something about the patient's assessment of his own adequacy in respect to a particular important part of his state of being. It is that self-assessment which gives rise to anxiety, depression, and other symptoms. We remarked earlier that a person evaluates his on-going lived time in accord with his assessment of his own adequacy, and that this affective assessment of the self links present circumstances with future outcomes on the basis of past outcomes in similar situations.

Formulation of the central issue in these terms also exposes its genetic and adaptive relevance. Through it one recognizes what the patient has been struggling with all his life, how he has tried to master it, and the unrelenting pain he has suffered nevertheless. The chronic pain, which originated in early life, can be identified as a response, as a variety of feeling and understanding, from the child's perspective, which is both correct and distorted. Thus, it invariably includes feelings of helplessness, separation, and abandonment. A degree of helplessness is the lot of every child insofar as control by the adult is inevitable. The pain of separation with its accompanying sense of abandonment is equally inevitable since, even in the best of early circumstances, separation is never achieved without pain. The multiple repetition of these experiences is a given for every human being. In some, the adaptive means devised by the ego to confront these painful repetitions are reasonably successful. The adaptive means of those who come to us for help have always been relatively unsuccessful; that is, the pain has always been more, rather than less, unrelenting.

To put it another way, the coping adaptive style is a device for diminishing pain and increasing pleasure. The repetitive experiences of pain, however, eventually invade the adaptive mode, and the person comes for help when that mode (and therefore he) is threatened by the eruption of previously warded-off aggression. The precipitating event is, in truth, the final blow that simply cannot be tolerated.

Some may feel that too much emphasis has been placed on the present and chronically endured pain. Our aim is to instill a way of thinking about, listening to, and empathizing with the patient in a way that reaches out to his or her major *affective* life experience. Few, if any, of our problems arise out of the "glad" feelings in life; most surely arise out of the "mad," "sad," "frightened," "guilty" feelings.

The statement of the central issue in the terms we have been describing is readily understood and accepted by the observing, rational ego. It stimulates the recall of affective experiences that are directly or indirectly related to the central issue. It informs the patient that the therapist is sensitively attuned to the patient's inner statement about himself. It becomes a source of considerable reassurance to the patient that the therapist can be trusted. The rapid establishment of a working alliance follows. *The goal of time-limited psychotherapy is to foster, to the degree possible, the resolution of the patient's chronic pain; to change his persistently negative self-image.* The patient's presenting symptoms or complaints will be diminished or entirely relieved through the resolution of the central issue. Symptom relief is a by-product of the process rather than its goal.

Clearly, in any brief therapy, the necessity for a sharply delineated entry into the patient's problems is paramount. Having made such an entry, the next task becomes a formulation of the process that will lead to successful resolution of the patient's complaints. It may be helpful, at this point, to remark on the differences and similarities between the methods of Sifneos,[1] Malan,[2] and Mann.

Both Sifneos and Malan have very specific criteria for selecting patients, especially emphasizing high motivation for change, demonstrated ego strengths, intelligence, and possession of relationship skills. In addition, the patient must be able to verbalize a focal problem. Sifneos carefully delineates the treatment focus in the course of the evaluation interview(s) in terms of what appears to be the conflict that the patient is experiencing with the important person or persons in his life, either directly or as a displacement onto others. His aim is to reach an agreement with the patient that this conflict is in fact the important problem that the patient wishes to pursue in treatment. Regardless of the patient's presenting symptoms or stated problems, Sifneos appears to aim at locating and formulating the patient's feelings about others. The central dynamic is the presence of an unresolved Oedipal conflict. Although feelings about the self inevitably emerge in the course of treatment, the therapist's goal is the relief of the patient's problems through interpretation of past and present events, as well as the transference, in direct or derivative Oedipal terms. Further, the criteria for selecting patients indicate a level of psychological intactness that allows the therapist to induce anxiety directly and from the start without undue concern about crumbling defenses or premature termination of treatment. Sifneos describes himself as an un-

[1] P. E. Sifneos, *Short Term Psychotherapy and Emotional Crisis,* Harvard University Press, Cambridge, Mass., 1972.

[2] D. M. Malan, *The Frontiers of Brief Psychotherapy,* Plenum, New York, 1976.

emotionally involved teacher. His approach is provocative and his aim is to teach the patient new and better ways of solving his problems.

Malan arrives at the focal problem through extensive interviewing and psychological testing. He does not inform the patient of the focus directly; rather, he establishes its validity by the nature of the patient's responses to interpretations, which are made at the very first opportunity. The interpretation may immediately focus on the transference to the therapist. From the start, attention is paid to the interpretation of the patient's conflicts in terms of the felt conflict between the patient and parent(s) (or between the patient and a displaced object in his current life) and between the patient and the therapist in his Oedipal transference role. Malan and Sifneos share the same thinking and technique in this regard.

Burke et al.[3] liken Sifneos's method to "a schoolmaster seeing through the excuses and alibis of his recalcitrant pupils." Malan's approach "is more like a senior lecturer . . . he is more didactic, less intense as he proffers interpretations to weave together present and past." Malan sets a termination date at the outset, with the number of treatment sessions varying from twenty to sixty or more, depending on the patient's needs. Sifneos has not paid attention to termination as a specific phase of the treatment; treatment ends when the patient feels he has made the necessary changes. Both Malan and Sifneos consider insight the curative element in their work.

The major differences between the Malan-Sifneos model and the Mann model emerge from the latter's specific limitation of time and the particular method for formulating the central issue. Thus:

1. Our criteria for case selection are lower than the Malan-Sifneos criteria, in some respects very much lower. On the a priori assumption that the patient who comes to us for help is already sufficiently motivated to change, we do not regard a statement from the patient of his wish to change as necessary. Further, the patient's motivation for change will be enhanced or diminished to the extent that the therapist appreciates the intensity of the patient's initial anxiety and can contain that anxiety in the initial interviews. An investigative approach that seeks to uncover recurrent painful events that affected feelings about the self becomes, at the same time, an effective means for diminishing frightening fantasies about the nature of the encounter with a therapist. Ego strength is determined primarily by assessing the patient's capacity to tolerate loss (as revealed in his history) rather than by assessing a wider variety of ego assets. Locating

[3] J. D. Burke, Jr., Henry S. White, and L. L. Havens, "Which Short-Term Therapy? Matching Patient and Method," *Archives of General Psychiatry*, vol. 35, 1979, p. 178.

a focal problem is the therapist's responsibility, but it requires a patient who can speak coherently about himself.

2. Our method is an empathic-clarifying-interpretive one in which insight, cognition, and affective experience all share in the outcome. Almost all transference interpretations are confined to the termination phase of treatment, when the central issue has become the paradigm of the transference. We will return to this point later.

Burke et al., in speaking of our kind of central issue (and in comparing the models of Sifneos, Malan, and Mann), remark:

> [Mann's] means of posing a central issue differ greatly from the teacher, who wants to impart new self-knowledge, and the director, who wants to provide a new, corrective experience that will be of immediate use to the patient. . . . The central issue, derived from past responses, also makes possible a prediction about the patient's response to the upcoming separation crisis of termination. . . . Furthermore, by seeing and feeling the past in the present, he gains a sense of connectedness.[4]

Posing the central issue as we have described it bypasses, for the time being, the exposure of the patient's felt conflicts toward others. Instead, it directs the patient's attention to his feelings about himself. Formulation in terms of direct expressions of conflict tends to increase defense and resistance automatically (hence unconsciously); the pressure on the patient to face up to the conflict may well increase the patient's inclination to agree with the therapist in order to please him and prevent further anxiety arising out of unconscious and conscious fantasies inherent in the conflict situation.

The central issue, as formulated in time-limited psychotherapy, does not confront the patient's projections or externalizations, and thus effectively dampens any expectation that the therapist may blame the patient. The question of guilt and innocence is not an issue at this time. It is common in treatment for the therapist's kindly expressed interventions consistently to be experienced by the patient as criticism and accusations. The central issue should short-circuit the patient's natural readiness to become defensive and resistant. The patient will become aware of his conflict with others soon enough in the course of treatment, but at a point when his trust in the therapist is firm and the alliance even stronger.

Further, if the patient population is primarily from the educated middle or upper classes, one can expect the excessive use of intellectualization at the expense of affect and experience. The central issue, expressed in terms of the patient's chronic pain and negative self-image, induces a treatment experience that rapidly becomes intensely affective for both

---

[4] Burke et al., op. cit., p. 179.

patient and therapist. The defensive distance between patient and therapist is soon dissolved.

3. In time-limited psychotherapy, reunion and separation become the central dynamic and, because reunion and separation recur throughout life, all levels of development are included. In long-term psychotherapy and psychoanalysis, when a termination date is agreed on, Oedipal conflicts tend to disappear in favor of the separation and loss problem, with its regressive and maturational impact. Better resolution of the separation-loss problem leads to a greater sense of self and greater independence, both of which affect Oedipal problems to the extent that they involve the same issues. While Oedipal problems are sexual at the core, they are not independent of earlier developmental problems nor need they be approached only in terms of libidinal-aggressive fantasies. Rangell[5] notes, "While psychoanalytic theory achieves an elegant parsimony in condensing the multiple anxieties to the two basic ones of separation and castration, it also leaves room for the infinite variations in their external manifestations."

Some may question our claim that successful work can be done in twelve sessions on a pregenital problem of profound significance (separation and loss), citing the work of Sifneos and Malan, who deal with clear-cut Oedipal problems that are presumably less severe. We emphasize, however, that separation and loss are never fully mastered by anyone; that people who come for help, regardless of their psychological state and diagnostic label, have failed at such mastery. We state that life consists of a never-ending series of reunions, separations, and losses. In fact, all changes in the biopsychosocial complex of human life experience are experienced as separations and losses, even when the change is for the better. Given an order of priorities among neurotic (and therefore unconscious) problems, our position is that those which arise from separation and loss are more global in their impact than Oedipal problems. Separation and loss problems include and transcend Oedipal conflicts without concentrating on them specifically. We are very much aware of the presence of Oedipal fantasies in our patients, but we choose to view them in terms of the central issue rather than as sexual-aggressive-guilty fantasies about parents or their representatives.

One may counter with the statement that Oedipal problems are never fully mastered, either, and that they are encountered repeatedly throughout life. Oedipal problems are, in fact, subtler and more readily displaced, sublimated, denied, repressed, and otherwise strenuously pre-

---

[5] L. Rangell, "On Understanding and Treating Anxiety and Its Derivatives," *International Journal of Psycho-Analysis*, vol. 59, 1978, p. 229.

vented from entering consciousness. The basic Oedipal anxiety, castration, never enters consciousness in the intact person. The conscious, affective experience of castration in men or women can only be found in states of acute psychotic decompensation. Castration anxiety is experienced consciously in both men and women (more so in men) in the feeling that the self is inadequate, defective, inferior, weak, or in a total devaluation of the self.

We propose, therefore, that our kind of central issue, with its time, affects, and self-image enclosed in a specific time span, provides an empathic-clarifying-interpretative framework for approaching problems that permeate all layers of development (self and structural) and that noxiously persist in the patient's ongoing life. Attention to the separation-loss axis and its effects on the self provides a means, over a short time span, of bringing about changes in ego and superego, in the inseparable connection between these structures, and in the concept of the self to a modest but clearly helpful extent. Mann's treatment model accommodates the same kind of patients treated by Sifneos and Malan but goes further in allowing for the treatment of a broader range of psychiatric problems.

Finally, in this connection, long experience in working through Oedipal conflicts in psychoanalysis allows one to question the feasibility of resolving them in short-term psychotherapy. In psychoanalysis, detailed work over a long period of time is required to bring the Oedipal conflicts into meaningful terms. A transference neurosis must be established in order to overcome the powerful resistance not only to recognizing but also to experiencing emotionally the implications and multiple derivatives of the Oedipal situation. Anything less is apt to be an intellectual experience lacking the necessary accompaniments of *felt* wishes and *felt* fears, which together with the cognitive recognition can make for a genuine maturational experience.

The combination of our time limit and our central issue cannot but help bring to the forefront of the treatment process the major plague that human beings suffer privately: namely, *the wish to merge with another but the absolute necessity of learning to tolerate separation and loss without undue damage to one's feelings about the self.* The statement of the central issue in our terms is, in effect, a paradigm of the transference that will ensue. Its aim is to enable the patient to recognize and affectively experience the origins and vicissitudes of the pain that has led to a maladaptive self-concept and thus to maladaptive behavior.

Let us proceed to practical matters: how the central issue is actually formulated for presentation to the patient, followed by a number of clinical illustrations.

The statement of the central issue has three parts. The first consists of the therapist's recognition of the patient's active, coping efforts to gain recognition and satisfaction of his need. The second recognizes the patient's failure and his feeling that he is a victim, i.e., his feelings about himself. The third states that how the patient came to feel this way about himself will be the work of treatment.

Case 1

A 32-year-old unmarried woman gave the presenting problem of feeling increasingly unable to perform creatively at her job. This difficulty had been going on for over a year, and she felt that she had been kept on the job only because of her considerable tenure. One year earlier a close girlfriend had killed herself, and shortly thereafter a male friend had likewise committed suicide. At about the same time, she had spent long hours with another girlfriend in an effort to prevent her from destroying herself. She felt that in some way she had been partly responsible for these "catastrophes." During the past six months her lover had also become depressed, and the patient had come to feel that she had at long last come to a real insight about herself. It was that she had a need to keep people dependent on her in the same way her father had always kept her mother totally dependent on him. She felt that this characteristic might have something to do with the terrible things that had been occurring. As a result, she feels incompetent at work, depressed, confused, and acutely anxious to learn more about herself.

Further investigation disclosed that her father was a successful businessman in a distant state. Mother was a full-time housewife. The patient had very strong feelings about her mother "deteriorating." By this she meant that mother's chronic back pain fostered dependence on father and barred her from pursuing her own interests; instead, she was forced. into what, in the patient's eyes, were degrading, petty social activities.

At age 14 the patient was sent to boarding school, where she was intensely lonely and homesick. It was an all-girl school that she had not wished to attend, but she felt unable to express her own wishes to her father. With the help of a schoolmate, she managed to finish school. In her third year of college, an intense preoccupation with what her parents would think and do if they knew about her private life was followed by an inability to do her work, and she "fell apart." She left school, returned home, and was in psychiatric treatment for about a year. She then returned to school and completed her studies. In the year that she was at home, she more or less secluded herself. Treatment was terminated when it was thought that she simply could not make use of it. After graduation from college, she returned home and met a foreign man who was temporarily stationed at a nearby industrial plant. She intended to marry him. However, when her parents learned that the marriage would result in her moving to a foreign country, they dissuaded her from marriage. She then came to Boston and began her present employment some years ago.

She remarked that she had never been able to talk about her feelings for her parents, not even in her first attempt at therapy. She felt that everything she did was determined by whether her parents approved or not. At times, especially in the past, she had had thoughts of suicide. It is important to note that she came from a fundamentalist background in which guilt and sin played a prominent role in life. As a result of her parents' restrictions and prohibitions, she suffered enormously from guilt and a sense of "badness." The extent to which her parents exercised control over her was manifest in their refusal to put up with her wearing casual clothing. Seen in a second interview one week later, she told of having suffered severe back spasms requiring narcotics for relief during that one-week interval. She was aware of the connection between her talking to me about her parents, her mother's back pain, and her own.

Out of this data, it was apparent that this woman had made very strenuous efforts to separate herself from the overwhelming presence of her parents and had endured a good deal of loneliness and despair in the years since her flight to Boston.

What was the central issue? Her depression? Her guilt? Her sinfulness? Her anger toward her parents? All these were important but vigorously defended against insofar as her feelings about their origins were concerned. She was intellectually aware of her dependent needs; her feelings about them were obscured by her depression and guilt.

The central issue was posed in terms of (1) her coping and adaptive efforts and (2) the chronic pain. Thus, the problem and work of therapy was stated as follows:

> You have made strenuous and successful efforts to be independent, and yet you have also always felt the pain of longing.

She responded with a surprised "Yes," and then, noting that I had said nothing about what she was longing for, added that she was probably afraid to know what it was. I agreed and added that during the twelve sessions we would focus on determining the object of her longing.

Eventually, in the course of treatment, we learned that her longing was to achieve reunion with her parents, to please her father and to be loved by him, a task that she had felt was impossible in childhood and adolescence. She appreciated that now, as an adult, her relationship with him had to be negotiated in entirely different terms. Her passive longings, distorted as they were by her intense fear of her father, had seriously interfered with her relations with men in her adult life.

Case 2

A 25-year-old married man came to the emergency room complaining of depression, severe anxiety, and suicidal impulses. He was seen briefly and referred to the psychiatry clinic. There it was learned that he had seriously considered suicide several weeks before. He had then thought about the effect his suicide would have on his wife and had stopped. Another of the patient's concerns was his hair-trigger temper. For about two years there had been episodes of thundering anger touched off by some seemingly slight remark by his wife; at times he had even struck her. The last such episode had frightened and depressed him so much that he had sought help.

The patient was born in the Midwest and never knew his father, who had abandoned his mother before the patient's birth. His mother gave him to her parents, with whom he spent the next eleven years. One day he learned that the woman who lived down the street, whom he had always known as his sister, was in fact his mother. He asked to live with her and did so for one year. Mother had remarried and had two children by her second husband. The patient was sorely hurt when mother was explicit about his standing in that household; he was number three rather than number one. As her oldest son, he had assumed that he would be number one. The patient claimed that mother allowed seconds in food to all but him. One year with his mother was enough; he returned to his grandparents' home, where he remained until he completed high school and hit the road. He was grateful to his grandparents for providing a home for him but recounted his misery when both of them were drunk for days at a time, leaving him to shift for himself as best he could. During those years he got into minor scrapes with the law, and such episodes became more frequent when he was on his own.

After much wandering, he recalled sitting at the side of a highway in the Far West and suddenly exclaiming to himself that he was "tired of being a shit bum." He then headed east, to the Boston area, where he found a job that really suited his needs. Steadily employed and doing well, he decided to visit his mother, who had since moved to the South. This attempted reunion was partially successful.

He returned to Boston and moved on to a better job in the same field, where he met his wife. While he was courting her, he learned that his mother was in the hospital with cancer and he rushed south to see her. He married about six months before his mother died; it turned out that he had known about his mother's cancer when he first met his wife. He was at his mother's bedside when she died, and his greatest sorrow was that he had not been able to show her how successful he was in both his marriage and his career. The unwanted son could not enjoy his sweet revenge.

The patient's marriage was a good one except for his temper outbursts which, significantly, were now noted as beginning with the death of his mother. In the preliminary interview, the patient also remarked on his readiness to cry whenever he thought about his mother, even though almost three years had elapsed since her death.

The patient presented himself as a somewhat ebullient young man, overcheerful and clearly eager to come across as a most acceptable and pleasing person.

One could have chosen the insufficiently mourned death of his mother, his temper outbursts, or his depression and anxiety as a central issue or focus. It was evident, however, that the intensity of his rage at his mother, as seen in the displaced attacks on his wife, would be vigorously defended against. Moreover, any attempts to get at that rage too directly might precipitate a loss of control in a man whose history included some difficulty with impulse control. The nature of the chronic pain became clear not only from the patient's history but also in a current work conflict. There, as he put it, he "broke his ass" to please, to gain some recognition, which never seemed to be forthcoming.

The central issue was stated as follows:

> You seem to be a decent kind of man and you have tried to please others, and yet you feel and you have always had the feeling that you are not wanted.

Recognition was given to the man's strivings, to his mode of adaptation to the persistent pain of feeling unwanted; the pain itself was verbalized and the task of treatment was clarified.

Some other examples of statements of the central issue:

> You have always worked so hard to make things better, but what hurts you and has always hurt you is that no matter how hard you try, you end up feeling that you are the loser.

> You have always given of yourself to so many others, and yet you always feel that you are both undeserving and unrewarded.

> You have devoted yourself so completely to your husband and children, and yet you never lose the feeling that you are inferior and inadequate.

Case 3

As another clinical illustration, we present the highlights of the first interview with a 42-year-old woman. She is preoccupied by fear for her family's safety: if her husband or children are late in returning home by even a minute or two, she panics with thoughts about their being killed. To appease her, they usually make certain to call her about any delay in their return home. She has the terrible fear that she will be left alone with total responsibility for whoever is left of her family. She has no such concerns if the whole family is traveling together, but she is almost paralyzed with anxiety when her husband has to fly to another city on business. Often her anxiety is free-floating, without content, on these occasions. She often has dreams that she describes as "sad"; for example, she has lost a book or her briefcase, or she and her husband are at a party and he goes off and doesn't return. She comes for treatment now because her husband says she is driving them all crazy.

She recalled an early memory of going with her father on a business errand. He parked the car and left her sitting in it. A man came out, entered the car in front of her, and drove away. She was stricken with the thought that the man was her father and had left her. When she was 5 years old, her family moved to another part of the country. Her busy father came home only on weekends. Her mother, a housewife, was described as a good mother although she suffered from recurrent depressions following a six-month hospitalization when the patient was 16. Since then the mother has been in and out of treatment and has had some courses of electroconvulsive treatment. The patient felt that she had escaped the worst effects of a depressed mother by leaving home for college. She noted that, despite her depression, mother was always available to her and could always put up a good front of humor and charm. (The patient's behavior in the interview was very much of this kind.)

After college, she moved to a large city where she obtained a job at an institution; there she had her first love affair. When marriage became a serious consideration, the man told her that he had a chronic malignant disease of the type that could remain in remission for many years or return at any time. The patient sought and received counseling, which, she felt, pointed up her dependence. She thereupon decided that the independent thing to do would be to marry, and they did. Shortly after the marriage, a recurrence of the husband's illness was successfully treated and they decided to have a baby.

Several weeks before her delivery, her father died of a malignancy. Not long after their child was born, recurrences of her husband's illness began and continued until his death four years later. Everyone marveled at her capacity to manage the prolonged agony and commented on her heroism. Her mother remarked on how little the patient cried.

She remained with her baby in the home she had had with her husband for another three years and was then invited to live in the Northeast. There she met a widower whom she married that same year. She has been very happy with her second husband, with whom she had another child.

In the interview one could clearly observe how she concealed depression with a somewhat exaggerated cheerfulness and outgoing manner. She emphasized her excessive conscientiousness and sense of responsibility. She carries a briefcase around with her since, if she has a free moment at her part-time job, she'll do some work relating to home affairs, and vice versa.

What would be an appropriate central issue in this case? Her anxiety? Her panics? Her depression? The frightening thoughts about loved ones dying? Delayed grief? Even in this one interview, it was possible to detect the significant recurrent event in her life to which she had responded with action, even heroic behavior, and a facade of cheery good humor and warmth. Her coping style had never sufficed, however, to undo or diminish the chronic pain.

The central issue was presented to the patient as follows:

> You have always feared that despite your best efforts you will lose everything.

Her response to this statement was a flood of tears and the remark, "It's true." When I gave her the treatment proposal, outlining the time of each session and the date of the final meeting, she promptly took out her work book and wrote the termination date in it. She said that she writes everything in that book—appointments, books she should read, things to buy—all in the service of not losing anything.

The central issue is clearly discernible in the patient's life story and requires only that the therapist bend his efforts to understand how, in the light of the data, this patient must feel about herself; how she has coped and how the pain has persisted nevertheless. Also, note that the central issue has a life over time, beginning when the patient was 5 years old and continuing to the present. The central issue is also a paradigm for the transference that will soon emerge.

It may seem, from the above examples, that the central issues acknowledged by the therapist speak only to the presence of depression. That would be true if the presence of depression were assessed only by the word or words the patient uses to describe the affect he is experiencing. But the feeling that one is a loser, or inferior, or unwanted, or helpless may be accompanied by a predominance of depression, or anxiety, or—in most instances—a mixture of the two. Whether depression or anxiety will prevail depends as much on the patient's perception of himself in time as on his assessment of his adequacy in the face of some painful internal or external reality that has come to absorb his attention. That is, based on one's past experience, one must assess the ego's capacity to cope with or master the felt threat or challenge. If one concludes that the ego is inadequate, a painful state of tension arises within the ego and is experienced as a loss of self-esteem, a feeling of helplessness, or a narcissistic injury. Whether anxiety or depression then follows will be determined by the inner judgment one makes that, on the basis of past experience, he can cope with the threat and feels that he has a future—or whether the judgment is that he is unable to cope and is without a future.

No matter what else a patient may be suffering, the fact that he comes to us for help bespeaks the presence of anxiety, which always indicates concern about future uncertainties. This is the meaning of the signal function of anxiety which summons the ego to rouse its defenses. The temporal element is equally evident in feelings of guilt. Some guilty feelings have to do with events or behaviors that are past and are properly remembered with feelings of remorse (I did something wrong or bad). Feelings of conscience judge the future (I should or should not do such and such).

In effect, then, an important judgment made in the course of evaluation interviews is the extent to which the patient experiences himself as having a future. This judgment is derived as much from the data of the patient's life history as from his statement about why he sought help. The young man whose central issue concerned his feelings of being unwanted was clearly depressed. Nevertheless, his life story indicated a capacity for mobilizing anxiety that conveyed the potential for a future. In the case of the woman with free-floating anxiety, both anxiety and depression were present, and the central issue was stated in terms of her feeling herself to be a loser. In another, very anxious patient suffering from an acute phobic reaction (see Chapter 5), the central issue was stated in terms of feelings of helplessness. The limitation of affects available to us directs us to search for the presence of anxiety, depression, or a mixture of the two. The presence of depression without anxiety, depending on its intensity and accompanying vegetative signs, may warrant another kind of treatment.

This method of selecting the central issue allows the therapist to reach out to the patient in a way no one else has. As we have already noted, the central issue goes beyond the patient's feeling that the therapist seems to care or is an empathic person. Rather, the patient feels as if someone is beside and inside him and is offering to remain there to help. The fact that the therapist reaches in so deeply without being frightened, depressed, or disgusted, and is offering to remain there for the purpose of helping, arouses in the patient feelings of gratitude and trust that hark back to the earliest of human experiences.

Kohut's *Analysis of the Self* [6] has been influential in creating a new understanding of the developmental process that leads to a reasonably

---

[6] H. Kohut, *The Analysis of the Self,* International Universities Press, New York, 1971.

intact sense of self or to deviations or defects in that sense. His theory and treatment of narcissistic disorders, based on the concept of a separate developmental pathway of narcissism, have wide implications for the treatment not only of narcissistic disorders but also of other, less pathological states. Kohut places particular emphasis on the role of empathy in human life and describes it as the matrix of man's psychological survival. In a later publication,[7] he defines empathy in three ways: ". . . empathy, the recognition of the self in the other. . . . empathy, the expansion of the self to include the other. . . . and empathy, the accepting, confirming and understanding human echo evoked by the self."

The concept of the central issue as we have elaborated it has evolved independently of Kohut's work. It conveys very clearly an empathic understanding of the patient's state of being as the patient experiences and lives it. Through the statement of the central issue, the therapist says that he knows how the patient feels and has always felt. Further, the central issue spells out the aim of treatment: that the patient learn what in the course of his life led to such painful feelings about himself. Invariably, this kind of central issue addresses insults to the patient's narcissism. We are not at all suggesting that in time-limited psychotherapy one can probe the sources of the injury, of the felt victimization, as occurs in the analysis of narcissistic disorders described by Kohut and many who have followed him. We do suggest, however, that our central issue selection and therapeutic method approach the same kind of problem in a derivative manner for a patient population that is generally less disturbed than those with severe narcissistic disorders. (See Chapter 4 on case selection.)

A central issue, as described here, should become apparent to the therapist in anywhere from one to three or four evaluation interviews. Sometimes the experienced therapist can arrive at an accurate assessment of the central issue in one interview. We have observed that, depending on the therapist's experience, if the central issue still remains obscure after three or four interviews, the patient may not be a suitable subject for time-limited psychotherapy. The patient may be severely disturbed and wholly unable to make contact with his inner life or with the therapist. Or we may be dealing with the kind of obsessional patient whose major and almost single defense resides in a total investment in his intellect to the exclusion of his feelings. Although the patient may demonstrate, in the course of the interview, what appear to be feelings, he does not know what it is to feel something. In such patients, the active unconscious fantasy life that has dictated such a defensive position can best be made available through psychoanalysis.

---

[7] H. Kohut, "The Psychoanalyst in the Community of Scholars," *The Annual of Psychoanalysis,* vol. 3, International Universities Press, New York, 1973, p. 347.

In one such case, a patient of enormous intellectual capacity had been treated in long-term psychotherapy in another city without success. A major complaint was his inability to allow himself any kind of sexual relationship with a woman. He was ashamed to be a virgin at his age, and the threat to his masculinity had not only depressed him but had also unconsciously invaded his one reliable fortress—his intelligence. This was manifested in his declining ability to work, his growing sense that his intelligence was eroding, and his growing feeling that suicide was the only answer. A massive increase in homosexual masturbatory fantasies only served to heighten his anxiety, depression, and sense of humiliation.

In preliminary interviews, it was not possible to search out and extract the kind of central issue appropriate for time-limited psychotherapy with its aim of diminishing or relieving his chronic pain and thereby releasing his inhibitions. Psychoanalysis was suggested and the patient agreed. Over the next two years of analysis, it became possible to reach a host of fantasies as well as to undo much of the isolation of affect that had been so firmly encased in the supremacy of the intellect. The release and analysis of the fantasies, along with the liberation of affect, made it possible for him to achieve a sexual relationship with a woman for the first time. He simply could not have been reached in any other kind of psychotherapy.

Choosing the central issue in time-limited psychotherapy requires a particular effort by the therapist. It means gathering all possible data about the significant painful events in the patient's life and then compressing into one statement the affective experience endured over many years. It means, further, that the therapist must ask himself how the patient feels about himself given his particular history, and what kind of feeling must it be that he has probably never verbalized to himself, a feeling concealed behind a variety of symptoms or complaints as well as by a long-standing behavioral style. Extracting the central issue calls for a full understanding of the facts—their chronological relationships and their dynamic and unconscious meaning—along with a sensitive perception of the patient's *feelings* about himself.

The sense of time, the awareness of affects, and the uncertainties about the self—all these are highlighted in the process of time-limited psychotherapy, in which the work with the self must be accomplished in a relatively short, specified time. All three—time, affect, and self—are stated in the central issue formulated by the therapist. The aim of treatment is to undo the particular conscious and unconscious time bond to the past that has perpetuated a guiding fiction about a deficient sense of self in the present with expectations that the future will be no different.

As the therapist gains in experience, he becomes aware that the same kind of central issue is evident in many patients; or that the number and variety of statements of the central issue appear to be quite limited. The therapist may begin to wonder whether he is employing a gimmick, or whether he is simply fitting a number of patients into one kind of mold. In fact, it has already been suggested that so long as the central issue is formulated and presented as an affective statement, the variety of ways in which it can be stated is already markedly limited by the finite range of affects available to human beings. Thus, the repetition of the same kind of central issue does not in itself suggest an error by the therapist. Soon enough the patient will reveal the unique circumstances of his life that make clear the central issue as the gateway to his inner life, which is the exclusive experience of this one human being.

3

Time, The Central Issue, and the Theory of Therapeutic Change in Time-Limited Psychotherapy

As a background to understanding the effectiveness of time-limited psychotherapy, and before entering into a specific discussion of our clinical-theoretical position regarding normal development and the etiology of psychopathology, we will note our overall approach to the latter. We view the etiology of psychopathology from essentially four perspectives: (1) the structural hypothesis; (2) the theory of narcissism and the development of self-esteem; (3) object relations theory; and (4) the developmental perspective.

The structural hypothesis states that, in the presence of conflict between the various agencies of the psychic apparatus, one or another variety of symptoms or character deformations will develop. We view this hypothesis as providing the basic understanding of the etiology of psychopathology. As is apparent from Freud's writings,[1] however, it did not and could not explain certain aspects of psychopathology that have now been more clearly conceptualized and delineated. In other words, although Freud emphasized the importance of conflict between the

[1] S. Freud, "On Narcissism," *Standard Edition*, vol. 14, Hogarth Press, London, 1957 (first published 1914); "The Ego and the Id," *Standard Edition*, vol. 19, Hogarth Press, London, 1961 (first published 1913).

psychic agencies in the etiology of neurotic psychopathology, he did not focus heavily on structural conflict as a determinant of psychotic illness and certainly never rescinded his view of the role of narcissism in the etiology of severe disturbance.

Only recently have others, such as Kohut[2] and Kernberg,[3] stressed the importance of narcissism in the production of nonpsychotic illness. Indeed, many other writers now view the vicissitudes of narcissism in early life as one of the crucial determinants in some of the severer neuroses and so-called higher forms of emotional disturbance. We do not see any inherent contradiction between the structural hypothesis and a hypothesis that includes the vicissitudes of narcissism as important potential etiological factors in psychopathology. We are aware of the current controversy in the literature in which these perspectives are pitted against each other as competitive points of view. Our view is that they are complementary. The importance of this assumption will be noted further on.

Object relations theory implies that in the development of psychopathology, whether of Oedipal or pre-Oedipal origin, there has been an environmental failure at least equal to constitutional or biological contributions. We have never seen a patient in psychiatric or psychoanalytic practice who has not been subjected to a failure in the environment; usually it is related to the behavior of one or both parents or to accidents of fate, such as the birth of younger siblings or the death or illness of parental objects. In the Oedipal area, we know that the seductive or over-competitive parent can be the direct cause of overwhelming conflict that leads to symptom formation. In the pre-Oedipal area, failures of mothering and fathering can lead to disturbances in such areas as the development of stable, healthy self-esteem.

In almost all patients, the transference development in time-limited psychotherapy will reflect pre-Oedipal and Oedipal parental failure. In the transference, the patient relives reunion with and separation from that parent who has failed the patient and who is therefore regarded with ambivalence and guilt. Resolution of these feelings within the transference is responsible for the patient's improvement. In therapy, the patient gets a second chance to reunite and separate in an adaptive way. Thus the broad view expressed in this volume: that the major plague of human beings is the simultaneous wish to merge with another and the absolute necessity of learning to tolerate separation and loss without undue damage to feelings about one's self. (This statement does not

[2] H. Kohut, *The Analysis of the Self*, International Universities Press, New York, 1971.

[3] O. Kernberg, *Borderline Conditions and Pathological Narcissism*, Jason Aronson, New York, 1975.

imply that we believe all psychopathology to be rooted in the first eighteen months of life.)

With regard to the developmental perspective, we believe that it has added a new dimension to how one views psychopathology and its amelioration or resolution. The developmental model dates back at least to 1905, when Freud published his "Three Essays on the Theory of Sexuality,"[4] but obviously it has since been elaborated and expanded on by many writers. Basically that elaboration stresses the notions of progression and regression, and it implies that if a specific conflict or developmental hurdle is overcome through psychotherapy (or by any other means), "normal" maturation will follow.

To cite an example in classical terms: the anal regression that results from a neurotic Oedipal fixation will cease when the Oedipal guilt has been resolved. To use Knight's[5] famous military analogy, in which soldiers equal libido, once Oedipal guilt is resolved, the major units of the army can move forward from the rear (anal libido) to the front lines (genital libido). This hypothesis significantly questions more classical views, such as those of Glover[6] in regard to inexact interpretation; Glover believed that every tributary of the neurotic conflict must be unearthed for significant and permanent progress to be made. As practicing psychoanalysts, we feel strongly that there are a great many patients for whom this "unearthing" is the treatment of choice. In these patients, the neurosis has become so embedded that it is impossible for significant progress to occur by removing one developmental hurdle.

In a significant number of patients, however, the removal of one difficulty can lead to powerful changes, as reflected in Knight's analogy. Indeed, the developmental perspective provides a significant theoretical underpinning for explaining how time-limited psychotherapy can produce lasting improvement in so short a time without emphasizing the direct experience of instinctual wishes as they relate to Oedipal and pre-Oedipal infantile drives. With this introduction, we now turn more specifically to the clinical theory of time-limited psychotherapy.

In time-limited psychotherapy, we emphasize the special importance of time as a means of relating the relatively short duration of treatment to the limitation of regression and subsequent short-circuiting of infantile

[4] S. Freud, "Three Essays on the Theory of Sexuality," *Standard Edition,* vol. 7, Hogarth Press, London, 1953 (first published 1905).

[5] R. Knight, "Borderline States," in *Drives, Affects, Behavior,* ed. R. Loewenstein, International Universities Press, New York, 1953.

[6] E. Glover, *The Technique of Psychoanalysis,* International Universities Press, New York, 1955.

expectation. Regression is a potential hazard in any therapeutic process. The more indefinite the length of therapy, the more likely the development of an underlying, fixed maternal transference in which an unconscious reunion with the early mother takes place. Because of the power of such a transference, with its promise of uninterrupted gratification, security, and indeed, immortality, the patient refuses to give up that for which he came to treatment in the first place—that is, his symptoms, whether they are typically neurotic, behavioral, or related to disturbances in self-image. Prolonged therapeutic stalemates may occur, with the patient unconsciously fighting improvement in order to ward off the dreaded termination, which in turn reinvokes the reality principle. As the ego anticipates termination it faces reality, and as it faces reality it must confront separation, an end to the timeless state, and a painful confrontation with aging and death.

While this process takes place with more or less success in every child, in our patients it has usually occurred with less success. Indeed, for a child to grow up and confront reality, to renounce infantile wishes and replace them with more aim-inhibited ones, and finally, to accept mortality, it is necessary to strike a bargain with life. That bargain involves the promise of future gratification as the price for renouncing the old gratification. In many of our patients, the road has been littered with broken promises and unending disappointments. They will accept no more promises and make no new bargains. Growing up the first time was hard enough; betrayal will not occur a second time. Thus, in some longer-term therapies, patients who have regained the childhood mother or found a new and better one are less likely to risk disappointment again. Only in such longer-term psychotherapies as intensive psychoanalytic psychotherapy or psychoanalysis are patients willing to try separation following conflict resolution. Even then they do so with trepidation and uncertainty, and many fight change to the bitter end. Only when they can believe again in the promise of future gratification, and this time with more confidence, are people willing to "grow up" a second time. Reality demands and treatment must aim at helping the patient recognize that his future gratification is up to him rather than others.

How then does time-limited therapy compare with psychoanalysis, with other brief psychotherapies, and with some of the longer-term psychotherapies? In making comparisons, we will focus mainly on the issue of regression and the state of timelessness in order to develop the clinical theory of time-limited psychotherapy, including its therapeutic effectiveness, with more conceptual clarity.

At the start, we will make what may appear to be a bold statement: time-limited psychotherapy is the only brief therapy that aims at both a dynamic and genetic experiential appreciation of the conflicts involved in the guiding fiction about the self in the context of powerful transference reactions which in turn reflect intense childhood wishes toward primary figures. We now turn to some clinical illustrations.

Case 1

A 47-year-old homosexual man came to treatment because of a severe depression following the breakup of his relationship with a much younger man. The patient was the older of two children. His brother, who was six years younger than he, was killed while the patient was taking care of him. The patient, then 12, was filled with remorse and grief, as was his mother, who "never seemed to get over it." Nevertheless, the patient seemed to "forget it," so much so that this part of the history emerged only during the psychotherapy, rather than during the evaluation. Some time in his midteens, the patient realized that he was a homosexual and thereafter maintained homosexual relationships "of one sort or another."

About one year before the onset of his depression, he decided to leave his lover of twelve years' standing, a man of about the same age as the patient and in the same line of work. He left because he had fallen in love with a much younger man. The patient claimed, however, that he was still in love with his former lover the whole time he was with the younger man and was, in fact, astonished that he had chosen to leave his former relationship. Also noteworthy was the fact that he was surprised that he had fallen in love with this younger man, toward whom he felt little friendship. During the year before he entered psychotherapy, he felt confused, moderately depressed, and anxious. A few weeks before the evaluation, the younger man ended the relationship. The patient's depression thereupon intensified, and he had pronounced suicidal thoughts. Although he had the opportunity to move back with his former lover, he declined to do so for reasons that he could not understand.

The initial phase of the time-limited psychotherapy went smoothly: the patient's depression decreased and, concomitantly, his self-esteem rose. The central issue had been chosen to reflect his chronic sense of worthlessness, which he had tried to master through the relationship with the younger man. In the eighth session, however, he began—not unexpectedly—to regress. It was during this and later sessions that more data emerged about his younger brother's accident and the patient's immense guilt about it. Moreover, it became apparent that he felt that mother had never forgiven him and that one of his main wishes was to obtain her forgiveness. He had never felt that reaction from his father, whom he saw as a kind, understanding man. In the transference it became quite apparent that the therapist represented his mother and that the patient was seeking the same forgiveness from him that he had longed for from his mother. It must be emphasized that this yearning for forgiveness was deeply repressed, as was his enormous guilt about his brother's death. When these deep-seated feelings emerged in the transference, they were discussed at length with eventual resolution. The patient improved dramatically. His self-esteem rose considerably, his suicidal thoughts disappeared, and he gave up the relationship with the younger man, who, he came to understand, served as a replacement for his younger brother.

Case 2

A 35-year-old single, unemployed professional woman entered treatment because of chronic feelings of worthlessness, accompanied by pervasive suicidal feelings. The only child of middle-class parents, this woman described her relationship with both of them as chronically frustrating and disappointing. She found her mother cold and ungiving, her father demanding and critical. She felt her father had wanted a boy and was never satisfied with her. In her adolescence she described always trying to please him and never succeeding, although she had done well in school. In fact, she did quite well in college, went on to graduate school, and embarked on a professional career. During college, graduate school, and the succeeding years, however, she had always had difficulty with heterosexual relationships. She repeatedly became involved with unavailable men who made her feel inferior and who, for one reason or another, rejected her. When she finally came to psychotherapy at the age of 35, she felt hopeless, dejected, and pessimistic about her prospects of being helped.

The central issue was chosen to reflect her long-standing, deep sense of worthlessness associated with her relationships to both her parents. During the initial phases of psychotherapy, her self-esteem seemed to improve and she even entertained the possibility of going back to work, which she had given up voluntarily two years before entering treatment. She seemed to rely on the psychotherapist quite extensively. Although she would argue with him against herself when he supported her self-esteem, she seemed to respond to his encouragement and support. Moreover, it seemed that, unconsciously, she was arguing against him and herself in order to cover a profoundly positive transference, which was based on finally finding a "good" parent.

In the ninth session she rather suddenly made note of the time left in treatment. In spite of her steady, ongoing improvement she said she had again begun to feel hopeless and "begged" the therapist to continue the treatment beyond the twelve sessions. It was less the request to prolong the therapy and more the style of begging that was striking. Indeed, it became apparent that this style of begging was something that had been prominent in her life since childhood. She was used to "pleading and begging" with her boyfriends to remain with her. In fact, she had begged and pleaded with her father in the same way whenever he was critical or reproving. What became apparent was that she had developed a deep, positive, erotically tinged relationship with the therapist, who, she felt, was about to reject her even as her parents had. She had no awareness that she was relating to her therapist in this way, nor had she been aware that she was relating to her boyfriends as she had related to her father and perhaps her mother. It became clear from the history that she had expected her father to give her the maternal warmth and affection that her mother had failed to give her.

Time-limited psychotherapy lends itself to a rather deep but controlled regression that is useful for therapeutic gain. Such regression is made possible by: (1) the special way the central issue is chosen, presented to, and received by the patient; and (2) the time limit itself.

In respect to the first factor, the central issue as delineated by the therapist reflects deeply felt, long-standing barriers to the patient's happiness and fulfillment. More often than not the guiding fiction about oneself has to do with seemingly insoluble dilemmas, negative concepts of the self, or perceptions of the world and others that tend to make fulfillment seem impossible. Moreover, these dilemmas are ordinarily not clearly conceptualized in the patient's mind. They are preconscious and thus only vaguely experienced. What the patient has felt more keenly are various mixtures of helplessness and hopelessness.

The particular method of selecting the central issue, which technically may seem to be only a clarification, allows the therapist to reach out in a way the patient has probably not experienced since early childhood. The patient's feeling is one of being deeply understood, in reference not only to current difficulties but also to the way he has always felt. That the therapist can understand what seems like so much in such a short time gives the patient a feeling that the therapist has literally reached in. It is more than that the therapist seems to care, or seems to be an empathic person. The process is much deeper, and the patient feels as if someone had placed himself beside and in the patient and was offering to remain there to help. (The latter is crucial. We have never seen an instance where the therapist was experienced as intrusive or was viewed with suspicion.)

Because the therapist reaches in so deeply and is not frightened, depressed, or disgusted by what he sees, and is offering to remain there for the purpose of helping, and indeed is optimistic, the patient feels a deep gratitude and trust reminiscent of his earliest experiences. Every troubled human being wishes for the earliest of helpers—mother. It was she who came to the aid of the infant beset by frustration and helplessness; who, before ego boundaries were established, stood beside and inside the infant and allowed the infant inside her. With the help of mother, the infant finds a state of satiation and pleasure out of a state of diffuse, uncontrollable anxiety. The resultant feelings in the infant are the archaic forerunners of love and gratitude. It is this constellation that is unconsciously reawakened in our patients and that leads to hope and an intense, positive transference early in treatment. The old refusal to trust others and to make another attempt at a bargain with reality has been challenged.

One may ask why this process of "reaching in" is special to time-limited psychotherapy. Of course, empathy is an important ingredient in all psychotherapies, but here we lay claim to a unique form of empathic communication. In no other form of psychotherapy is a special attempt made at the beginning to link a profound notion about the self to factors of time (as duration) and intense affect. Thus, the central issue as posed includes a statement about the self, the length of time the patient has felt that way, and the intensity of his emotions. In our experience the length of time is almost universally stated and felt as "always," no matter whether the therapist and/or patient can temporally identify the significant pathogenic traumata. It may be possible to note that important etiological traumata occurred at a specific age or ages. Regardless, the patient very rarely states that he began feeling this way at this or that age; again it is felt as "always."

On reflection, this apparent contradiction readily becomes understandable. Powerful traumata, at least through adolescence, profoundly influence either unconscious guilt, or narcissistic equilibria, or, as is most often the case, both. Negative influences on either affect relationships to the primary internal objects, the parents. Since the relationships hark back to childhood, when the earliest introjections occur, objective time is obliterated (as far as affective experience is concerned) and the felt myth about the self is experienced as always having been there. This adds to the sense of hopelessness, for the patient cannot believe that something experienced so powerfully for so long will be easily removed. Thus, the affective result of trauma blurs time perspective, which in turn increases negative affect and results in a further sense of hopelessness—fueled by the "forever" quality of the pain—and therefore the impossibility of future resolution.

Because of this dynamic, our patients speak of an impossible past, an unhappy present, and a forbidding future, in which the pain of the past and present must be continued. It is because the central issue directs itself to just these factors that, in our experience, it is so effective. It includes the "always," the intensity of the pain, and the way in which the patient has experienced it and tried to adapt. As discussed earlier, the central issue produces an intense, positive transference with real and archaic features. In addition, the therapeutic alliance is intensely positive from the beginning, allowing more work to take place in a shorter time. The whole experience is analogous to the simple physics experiment in which one places a magnifying glass in the path of the sun. If an object is placed before the magnifying glass at its correct focal length, the heat from the sun is greatly intensified—sufficient, for example, to burn a piece of newspaper.

Phrasing the central issue so that it includes the above elements allows the patient to cathect it with very great intensity. Obviously, because not all aspects of this intensity are pleasant, the patient will attempt to diminish it in favor of a prolonged and gratifying relationship with the therapist, which seems to unite the patient with his earlier introjects and thereby undoes the guilt and old blows to his self-esteem—all without another separation. The patient attempts, as it were, to remove the magnifying glass, to reduce the painful intensity; in longer-term psychotherapy he usually succeeds. In psychoanalysis, such an attempt is analyzed as resistance. In other, less intense long-term therapies it is far more difficult to interpret the process as it occurs. More about this and the effects of the time limit will be discussed shortly.

Because of the therapist's early activity, initial phrasing of the central issue, and confidence that the patient can be helped, the patient develops an attitude of trust of an intensity that one does not ordinarily see so quickly in other treatment modalities. Although we have made note of the archaic forerunners of the trust, it should be emphasized that the ego has not suspended judgment in the establishment of this trust. It participates and sees a realistic basis for this trust, for the therapist has accurately and clearly stated the patient's lifelong affective problem. It is this aspect of the transference that keeps things together in the termination phase of treatment, when the more archaic transference is threatened and old disappointments reappear. This latter issue leads us to the discussion of the second factor mentioned before, the time limit itself.

It should be mentioned that, in and of itself, the time limit would have little value if it were not for the profound transference set in motion at the beginning of treatment. Various strategies for setting time limits on the therapy—whether they involve setting termination dates before or during therapy, or fixing the total number of hours, with the patient choosing the dates—have been and are being employed with varying degrees of success. In and of themselves they bear little relation to time-limited psychotherapy. Often their major aim is to limit regression and stimulate mobilization of the patient's adaptive capacities. While this aim is important in time-limited psychotherapy, it is only one ingredient among many.

Once the initial trust is stimulated, the time limit becomes of critical importance. Initially, all patients are to some extent disappointed with the time limit and, as will be seen, some refuse to enter treatment or leave early. Most patients, however, also feel significant relief, for another side of them does not wish to enter into another long-term relationship which, like earlier ones, might result in disappointment. Thus, paradoxically in these patients, who are a significant proportion of those seen, the time limit enhances trust and further stimulates old wishes, which are now transferred to the therapist—not in spite of the time limit but *because* of it. It is as if the patient said to himself, "Because it is only a short time, I can give it all I've got and see if I should try again [in life]. If it fails, because it is such a limited time, it won't hurt as much and I'll just go back to the way I was before."

Thus, in relating time—or more specifically, brief time—to the development of trust, we can say that any patient entering psychotherapy has a strong desire for improvement, which in turn relates to the abatement or removal of painful affect, i.e., anxiety or depression. In longer-term psychotherapies, the patient relates the amelioration or disappearance of symptoms to the length of psychotherapy. The longer the psychotherapy, then, the less trust there is initially. To put it another way, the longer one must wait for fulfillment, the more impatient and relatively hopeless one feels. We quote Hartocollis:[7]

> The stronger the wish, the more impatient one gets with the flow of time, which experientially represents the vehicle of getting to the sources of gratification—the means of achieving wish fulfillment. The stronger the wish, the slower the flow of time appears to be; and vice versa as the wish loses its urgency—and as long as there is a wish—time appears to move relatively faster.

Thus the time limit itself arouses hope in the patient based on very early and archaic expectations of wish fulfillment. This archaic mechanism is universal and, of course, has its roots in infancy, when the intervals between being alone and suffering frustration and helplessness, on the one hand, and feeling gratification and infantile omnipotence with mother's arrival, on the other hand, were crucial. This very interval profoundly affects later ego development, especially self-esteem, which in this context refers to the perceived capacity of the self to master present and

---

[7] P. Hartocollis, "On the Experience of Time and Its Dynamics with Special Reference to Affects," *Journal of the American Psychoanalytic Association*, vol. 24, 1976, p. 367.

future threats. With mother's arrival, because of fusion fantasies that make mother and infant one, the infant perceives an increase in his own capacities, which in turn increases his self-esteem. The process is the reverse of what happens in the "independence" of adult life, where so many view asking for and receiving help as a blow to their narcissism.

In time-limited psychotherapy, however, the rapidity of mother's arrival in the form of the therapist, who is experienced as being inside and beside the patient as mother once was, reawakens the old process and improves the patient's self-esteem. Such regression is truly in the service of the ego. It is, in fact, an ego regression in which boundaries between self and object are blurred for the purpose of ending a state of helplessness temporarily, and later more thoroughly through identification with the therapist in the termination phase of treatment.

In the preceding, the time of mother's arrival and the ability to anticipate the future are intimately linked. Thus again, the time limit in time-limited psychotherapy holds out the possibility of quicker relief of pain, which in turn produces optimism and a more powerful positive transference.

During the early and middle phases of time-limited psychotherapy, the therapeutic alliance and positive transference are very strong, not only because of the therapist's initial empathy but also because of the time limit itself. As we saw earlier, each factor potentiates the other. Therapeutic work initially proceeds at a very rapid pace, again because of the therapeutic alliance, the positive transference, and the knowledge that time is limited. Because of the great amount of therapeutic work done, symptomatic relief is quite rapid at this point, often startling to the observer and the patient himself.

During the late phases of therapy (often about the last one-third), regression does occur, as it would in any intensive psychotherapy or in psychoanalysis. It is here that the patient is again confronted by loss and, rather than lose the therapist, may develop symptoms again. Having experienced hope, he has felt he can try again to make a new, better bargain with reality. But when he confronts the reality of termination, to a large extent denied in the earlier phases of treatment, the threat of losing the therapist and thus the old primary object becomes so powerful that he retreats to a position close to the one he held on entering treatment.

Here again, the notion of time is of critical importance. Whereas in the earlier phases of treatment, the patient subjectively experiences the remainder of time in treatment as unrealistically long, in the final phase, the time of the last several sessions seems amazingly brief to him. Time seems to be flying by for the patient, not because there has been no realistic improvement but because he perceives the relationship to the therapist as rapidly coming to a close. Object ties (to the therapist), which unconsciously seemed so permanent, are threatened with dissolution. We quote again from Hartocollis:[8]

> The fact that a person is able to experience affect seems to signify that he still maintains his ties with the world of internal objects, the notion of time representing the vague awareness of such ties. The tentative nature of these ties tends to create the illusion that time is flying, is moving away from the self while the self remains immobile.

While Hartocollis is referring to the patient's relationship to his internal objects, in our opinion the same holds true in relation to external objects—in this case, the therapist. Moreover, we know that deep transference experiences profoundly affect one's relationship to one's internal objects. Indeed, if they did not, therapeutic progress probably would not occur. It is here that the patient's realistic trust, which was developed early in treatment, saves the day. Repeated interpretations linking the loss of the therapist with past losses and with past and present symptoms, misconceptions about the self, and maladaptive behavior lead to a more permanent reduction of the latter; the patient is now more confident of making it on his own. We repeat that this termination process is no different from that seen in other intensive psychotherapies or psychoanalysis, where strong transferences develop and distress reappears in the context of the termination phase, with one exception: in time-limited psychotherapy there is a great telescoping of the whole process.

To our knowledge, in no other brief therapy are the two critical factors—the presentation of the central issue and the setting of the initial time limit—built in as the significant therapeutic variables determining the effectiveness of the treatment. It is these that produce the profound, early positive transference–therapeutic alliance and the intense telescoping of the therapeutic process. For example, most crisis intervention techniques rely on rapid support with little, if any, conflict resolution and no real attempt to relate past and present. Other therapies call for a "focus," but leave out one or both of the critical factors mentioned. If there is a time limit, often it is not chosen until late in treatment. In our judgment, this approach leaves patients too uninvolved in the beginning and without a significant termination-phase regression, which is crucial for therapeutic consolidation and for the continued development of the patient's self-confidence after he leaves treatment.

Time-limited treatment does not attempt to compete with psychoanalysis, whose goals are much more ambitious. In analysis, conflict resolution is attempted at every level in the context of unlimited

---

[8] P. Hartocollis, "Time and Affect in Psychopathology," *Journal of the American Psychoanalytic Association*, vol. 23, 1975, p. 388.

time. In time-limited treatment, the goals are more modest; in the area of the central issue, however, a thorough reworking of the old conflicts is attempted in the context of telescoped time.

In comparison to other long-term therapies, time-limited treatment avoids some of their disadvantages, such as a pronounced but subtle and prolonged dependence on the therapist which, by unconscious mutual agreement, the therapist and patient never discuss. Indeed, such dependence is often difficult to pin down and define. In these cases, one often sees superficial understanding with only minor symptomatic relief rather than intense work leading to conflict resolution and true symptomatic relief. The patient becomes involved only enough to maintain the dependence and works only hard enough to continue the guise of psychotherapy. In these instances, unlike time-limited psychotherapy and other intensive psychoanalytic psychotherapies such as psychoanalysis, the regression is not in the service of the ego and is not therapeutic.

4

Case Selection

Most patients suitable for time-limited psychotherapy fall within the range of those having symptom and character neuroses. Not all patients with those diagnoses are likely to benefit, however. And there are some in the borderline or narcissistic spectrum who may achieve excellent results, albeit in more limited areas.

The most critical variables in determining outcome, which must be carefully evaluated during the assessment, relate to the strength of the ego and its capacity to allow for rapid affective involvement and equally rapid affective disengagement—the latter often being referred to as the capacity to tolerate loss. While the capacity to tolerate loss is an almost self-evident variable, the willingness to quickly invest importance in another person can be overlooked as a crucial factor. For example, schizoid characters ordinarily resist involvement. When they do become involved, however, termination results in either an exacerbation of their symptoms or a deepening rigidity of their character pathology owing to profound feelings of abandonment and consequent anxiety and rage, which the ego cannot tolerate.

In the neurotic spectrum, there are certain obsessional patients who so widely employ the defenses of isolation and intellectualization that their capacity for affective experience is quite limited; they too, therefore, cannot become rapidly involved. Here the capacity to tolerate loss is present, but the initial involvement—which makes the experience of loss possible in the first place, and therapeutically meaningful in the second place—is absent. In such cases psychotherapy may become twelve sessions of theorizing, speculation, and rumination. It ends as it began, with the patient frustrated and doubtful.

Also in the neurotic range are those hysterical patients who are able to tolerate loss but who are so unconsciously resentful of the prospect of it that they essentially refuse to become involved. While they may make a conscious attempt to work, psychotherapy becomes bogged down in their avoidance of the central issue and pseudo involvement in other issues, which serve to dilute the process and to set the stage for requests to prolong the therapeutic experience. While some of these patients wish to increase the number of sessions, others refuse time-limited psychotherapy at the outset. It is best not to challenge such a refusal. Still others in this group present a different pattern. They begin therapy, but instead of attending to the central issue, they concentrate on the qualities of the therapist, i.e., his capacity to listen, to "care," and to understand. What appears to be an intense transference involvement is in reality a hostile pseudo testing aimed at devaluing the therapist before the patient is devalued through termination, which is seen as a rejection. Repeated interpretations of the underlying issues often give the patient further ammunition to prove that the therapist does not "understand"; they are met with repeated denials. By the fifth or sixth session, when termination is even more intensely anticipated, these patients may leave therapy, feeling that both they and the therapist have failed. The following example illustrates the point.

A 22-year-old single woman entered time-limited psychotherapy complaining of chronic depression which began after the breakup with her boyfriend about one and a half years earlier. The older of two children born to middle-class parents, she complained that throughout her later childhood and adolescence she had felt lonely and generally devalued by both parents, who preferred her younger brother, on whom they showered admiration and attention. She, too, admired and praised him for his aggressive, competent style, comparing his good looks and personality to her own and finding herself "short" in both respects. Although she attended college and achieved good grades, she received little in the way of approval or support.

When she was 18 and in her freshman year of college, she had her first sexual relationship. The man she met and fell in love with was a high school dropout. Describing him as handsome and "tough," she admired his "cool," aggressive style. In spite of her achievements, she felt inferior to him and, although clearly exploited, she clung to him until he ended the relationship about fifteen months after it began. Although mildly depressed for a few months after the breakup, she continued to do well in school, where she found herself admiring and developing crushes on young, attractive professors who seemed "sharp" and forceful. In this context, she developed an intimate relationship with a young professor whom she found extremely intelligent and insightful. He would make comments about her personality that "penetrated" her facade and "zeroed in" on her "basic motivation." Although she felt humiliated and exposed, she enjoyed the power and accuracy of his comments and loved and clung to him all the more. About a year after they began the relationship he ended it, leaving her quite depressed and disconsolate. For the next eighteen months, she could think only of him and when she occasionally met him, she felt better, entertaining hopes of eventual reconciliation. Finally, soon after her graduation from college and about three months before she came to treatment, she realized that her hopes would not be fulfilled; the result was a more severe depression associated with profound feelings of worthlessness.

This patient demonstrates all the dynamics of a hysterical, masochistic character. Devalued by her parents in favor of her brother, she sought love objects for affirmation of herself, which could only be achieved by possessing the valued phallic male. Her envy of and rage at her brother were covered by powerful reaction formations that tended to idealize him—and later her lovers—still further. Rejection by her boyfriends resulted in a rupture of the narcissistic identification necessary for self-esteem and a threatened emergence of the original, more deeply buried envy and rage.

In the evaluation interview, the central issue that was chosen related to her low self-esteem and her quest for the ideal man, who would be more powerful and admired than she felt herself to be. At this interview, she accepted the central issue enthusiastically and without reservation. In the first two therapeutic interviews, she discussed the rejections by her lovers and her consequent feelings of worthlessness. She welcomed my interpretations relating the men to her brother and discussed her feelings of inferiority toward him.

By the third interview, however, she began discussing areas unrelated to the central issue. When I attempted to point that out, she showed signs of irritation. By the fourth interview, she began to question my "understanding" of her; she described certain words I had used as "not quite hitting the mark"; and, in general, she became contentious and devalued my interpretations and empathic ability. In the fifth interview, she announced she was leaving treatment both because I did not understand her and because she was critical of time-limited psychotherapy itself. She stated that such therapy was "too short" and hinted that she would remain in treatment if it were prolonged. At this time, she wanted to know more about me personally and felt resentful when I did not answer her questions but instead tried to understand with her the meaning of her request and the timing of its appearance in treatment.

Finally, I made an interpretation of her behavior: she was treating me as her boyfriend and parents had treated her; that is, she was retaliating toward them by devaluing me in the transference. Moreover, she was treating me this way because she anticipated termination, which she saw as rejection, and rejection was something she would have no more of. I pointed out that some confirmation for this interpretation lay in her hint that, despite my "not understanding" her, she was willing to remain in psychotherapy if I agreed to a more prolonged process. She reacted to the interpretation with interest and obvious signs of agreement. Because of this, she agreed to come for the next session, at which she announced that she completely disagreed with me and was leaving psychotherapy. As was typical, she offered no alternative understanding and would not state the reasons for her disagreement. She left after the sixth meeting.

Neurotic patients with strong dependent longings may also refuse to become involved, may attempt to prolong the treatment, or may leave early in anticipation of termination. It should be emphasized, however, that many dependent people can tolerate and benefit greatly from time-limited treatment. Such patients usually are aware of their dependency and have attempted to come to grips with earlier loss, although without success. Although they anticipate and fear another disappointment, they are also eager for help and are able to utilize and integrate the therapist's interventions.

Patients with narcissistic disorders ordinarily refuse time-limited psychotherapy, considering it far too little help for such important problems in such a significant person. Again, however, there are those with mild narcissistic difficulties who experience the twelve sessions as a challenge and who indeed work effectively during the treatment. It should be mentioned that they often require approval and "feedback" from the therapist to continue the effort. These patients can tolerate loss provided they feel they have done a "good job" in doing so.

So far, we have discussed those patients who have difficulty in becoming involved, some because they are fearful of the impending loss and others for different reasons. We now turn to those patients who not only are fearful of loss but absolutely cannot tolerate time-limited psychotherapy without severe regression. In this category fall the schizoid character, the manic-depressive and schizophrenic psychoses, and—for obvious reasons—other acute and chronic disorganizing psychoses. Mild psychotic depressions, however, must be carefully evaluated. Traumatic events may produce overwhelming but short-lived psychotic phenomena in a person with an otherwise well-functioning ego. When the meaning of the loss can be effectively related to the lifelong myth about the self, a central issue can be readily established and therapeutic work accomplished.

Some persons with the diagnosis of depressive character may pose significant therapeutic difficulties in time-limited therapy. In this situation, deep feelings of unworthiness in relation to oral longings and rage wreak havoc on the therapeutic alliance in that there is continual projection onto the therapist of the patient's profound inner self-devaluation and displacement toward him of rage that was originally directed at the ungiving mother. Time-limited psychotherapy may reproduce the early loss of the mother (now represented by the therapist) in an unworkable way. In some cases, although the "character" may not respond to time-limited psychotherapy, exacerbations of the depression can be successfully treated.

Similarly, people with typical borderline conditions cannot tolerate this form of treatment. Directly or through manipulation, these patients often seek direct gratification of early infantile wishes. When this aim is frustrated in the therapeutic process, they respond with chaotic and often self-destructive behavior. Fortunately, these patients tend to refuse the option of time-limited treatment; when they do not, they make every effort to prolong the therapy in the hope of achieving eventual gratification. These borderline patients, whom we have called "typical," are those who are prone to develop transference psychoses. There are, however, milder forms of borderline illness in which transference psychoses either do not develop at all or remain minor in intensity and duration. These patients do have ego deficits related to reality testing but, since they are less prone to develop severe transference distortions, they can develop a therapeutic alliance and work effectively in time-limited treatment.

Thus far, we have discussed those characteristics of the ego that are important for effective time-limited psychotherapy; namely, the capacity for rapid affective involvement and the capacity to tolerate loss. We have emphasized those traditional diagnostic categories, and the subgroupings within some, where we believe the ego does not have those necessary qualities. At the extreme, schizophrenic patients can neither become involved in treatment nor tolerate loss. Some obsessional types can tolerate loss but cannot become involved, whereas many borderline patients become intensely involved but cannot endure termination. Also mentioned were some examples of patients who have the potential to become involved and to tolerate loss but who, because of conscious and preconscious predilections, do not wish to participate. We now turn to those for whom time-limited psychotherapy is especially suitable.

Aside from the exceptions noted above, patients with a neurotic character structure are most likely to have the ego capacity for both rapid affective involvement and the toleration of loss. In the hysterical and obsessive-compulsive categories lie a host of dynamic issues that are amenable to time-limited intervention. Since failure to resolve triangular issues is central in these neuroses, symptoms or characterological difficulties frequently have Oedipal conflicts at their root. Thus, these patients may present with a variety of complaints ranging from anxiety and depression to conversion reactions or obsessive-compulsive symptoms. Characterological problems may be the presenting complaint. Repetitive, unsatisfactory love relationships, problems in work or school adaptation, or difficulty with peers may cause a person to seek help. Sometimes the complaint is subtler: the patient may only have experienced an increase in a long-standing discomfort, such as feelings of inferiority, without clinical signs or symptoms of depression. In spite of the subtlety, the same issues are present.

Aside from specific Oedipal-stage problems, these patients also often suffer from problems reflecting more general maturational issues related to the independence-dependence, separation-individuation, and activity-passivity dichotomies. Whether the etiology relates primarily to unresolved triangular conflicts, to maturational conflicts, or to an interplay of the two, a request for help is often made when an important psychological equilibrium has been broken, such as occurs when one enters a new phase of the life cycle or when one suffers a specific loss. Thus, entering college and/or leaving home, graduations, marriage and parenthood, one's children leaving home, the involutional phase—all present states of transition and loss where important equilibria are challenged and where symptoms may therefore develop. Let us turn to a clinical example.

A 19-year-old single college sophomore sought help because of periods of depression and anxiety that began in his freshman year, shortly after he arrived on campus from out of state. Although his grades did not suffer, he became increasingly immobilized and sought help.

The older of two siblings, the patient had had a very close, complicated relationship with his mother since his father's death when the patient was 5. At that time, he recalled saying to his mother, "Now, Mother, one good thing about Daddy not being here any more is that we can be closer than we could have ever been before." And indeed they seemed to be. Mother frequently told stories about father, played father's favorite music, encouraged the patient to read father's favorite books, and finally interested him in father's profession. She spoke of his values and beliefs and before too long seemed to have recreated her husband in the child. The patient, for his part, remained happy until he was "shocked" by mother's beginning to date during his adolescence and finally remarrying about two years before his symptoms began. In spite of her remarriage, however, the patient struggled in every way to remain the one closest to mother and, for the most part, he succeeded. He continued to confide in her and she in him, he demanded and won her frequent attention, and he sought and obtained her unending praise. He ignored his mother's husband.

Finally, on entering college, he began to experience periods of anxiety and depression. At such times he would call home and, once having reassured himself that mother was still close by, would feel better. Thereafter, the intervals between his periods of symptoms shortened, while his demands for reassurance intensified. The only respite he had was during the summer between his freshman and sophomore years, when he lived at home and felt happy again. When he began his second year, his symptoms returned in full force. By this time, phone calls and weekends home offered little relief.

From the above description, it may be noticed that there were two powerful issues to which his symptoms were related. The first involved his fury at being displaced by his stepfather, a displacement that ended his earlier Oedipal victory. The second involved strong anxiety connected with the maturational theme of independence-dependence. Both were precipitated by an age-appropriate transition in his life circumstances: leaving home and attending college. In other patients, however, these transitions are sometimes delayed and postponed for many years, resulting in either low-grade symptoms or none at all until such time as the wish to make a change occurs. For example, the decision to marry may be postponed until the fourth decade, and until then, a late adolescent lifestyle may predominate. When the person wishes to change because "time is running out," he may seek treatment.

While we have focused mainly on those classical neuroses especially suitable for time-limited psychotherapy, it should be mentioned that there are a host of other patients whose presenting difficulties are amenable to time-limited treatment. In these patients, the difficulties have their origins in periods other than that ordinarily associated with the classical neuroses. Thus, in spite of significant defects in mothering and the absence of an early "average expectable environment," many patients, for reasons not well understood, emerge with relatively intact egos capable of rapid affective involvement and of tolerating loss. Their presenting complaints almost always relate to vulnerabilites originating in early maturational failure. Careful diagnostic assessment is required to separate these patients from the typical borderline, narcissistic, or severe depressive characters mentioned earlier. Thus, each patient, regardless of his presenting complaint and early history, must be evaluated on his own terms without any preconceived prejudice or bias. Barring the clearcut exceptions that we have noted, careful assessment of the patient's life history in terms of his relative success in work and in relationships with others becomes an effective means for determining suitability for time-limited psychotherapy.

A word about the classical psychosomatic disorders. In general, persons with such psychosomatic illnesses as rheumatoid arthritis, ulcerative colitis, asthma, severe duodenal ulcer, and regional enteritis, have significant separation-individuation difficulties with a corresponding unavailability of affect. For mild psychosomatic illness, such as migraine, mild "functional" hypertension, and mild duodenal ulcer, time-limited psychotherapy can be attempted, but only after a careful evaluation of the patient's ego strengths, availability of affect, and capacity to tolerate affect. In these cases, a history of well-managed, meaningful object loss, at least at some point in the past, is essential if therapy is to be attempted.

5

Acute Phobic Reaction:
(I'm a Big Guy but I'm Scared)

The following case is one of three detailed descriptions of the process of time-limited psychotherapy to be presented in this book. We include the evaluation interview material, the formulation of the central issue, the offering of the treatment proposal, the beginning of the work, and the twelve sessions through to termination. A follow-up interview is also summarized. Annotated excerpts of dialogue from the treatment sessions serve to clarify the therapist's thoughts and therapeutic activity. Two other such cases are presented in Chapters 6 and 9. The cases presented in Chapters 7 and 8 are described in less detail. The reader will understand, however, that in all the cases the process is essentially the same.

Mr. T, a 32-year-old educator, had been assigned, with two female teachers, to a classroom consisting of five disturbed children, all suffering from impulse disorders. He had felt totally at a loss as to how to proceed with these children and had become intensely anxious. He "sweated it through" for one class session but was unable to return for subsequent ones. The mere thought of entering that classroom provokes an anxiety attack of classical proportions—perspiration, rapid heartbeat, a sense of dread, and "a great knot in my stomach."

Mr. T had studied and worked with many normal children in the course of his career. He suddenly recalled that when he had been a first-year graduate student he had decided that he should do some work with disturbed children and so had started a class with three such children. He quickly rationalized that he was becoming much too involved with their problems and dropped the project. On further recollection, it occurred to him that, in fact, he had suffered the same kind of anxiety with those children and had avoided a recurrence by returning to work with normal children. He had continued this work for ten years.

Mr. T was now on leave and had come to Boston both to study with Mr. Z, a scholar in his field, and to complete negotiations with another colleague, Mr. R, for a contribution to a series of books that Mr. T was editing. It was in his clinical experience with Mr. R that he had been assigned to the classroom of disturbed children. At the time of his referral, he had slightly more than two months before his leave ended, at which point he would return to his home base.

A review of his past history disclosed that, as a child, he had been big for his age, so that very early in high school his size commanded the attention of the football coach, who promptly put him on the football team. He felt unable to refuse although he knew that he was afraid of violent or uncontrolled behavior and had never been in a physical fight in his life. He differentiated physical and verbal fights; he has always been a ready contender in the latter. He was active in other high school activities and achieved notable success in another, more artistic, activity. He attended an excellent college, where he had a very good time at the expense of his studies, so that he was unable to fulfill parental hopes for a particular profession. He was admitted to graduate school, where he met his wife. They now have two children in what appears to be a very good marital and family relationship.

Mr. T's parents were business people, each owning a separate enterprise; they left for work early each morning and returned home in the evening. He remembered always being afraid to be left alone, even though a maid was present when the parents were out. He countered his fear by engaging in some kind of activity and would readily lose himself in reading. He contrasted this kind of uncontrollable situation (his parents leaving him every morning) and the discomfort he experienced at that time with his total comfort in engaging in research in his particular field. He controls that situation completely. He promptly sets up guidelines for the work to be done and "everything becomes predictable." In this connection, he recalled that when he goes to a strange city in the course of his work and has difficulty in finding his destination, he becomes scared. He was reminded again of his fear in the classroom of disturbed children and remarked that, though he obviously was not physically afraid of the children, he was terribly anxious about their uncontrolled behavior.

Enough data had been obtained in this evaluation interview to warrant the understanding that Mr. T was an obsessional man whose defenses protect him against the anxiety aroused by any kind of unstructured situation. The intense anxiety he experienced in the classroom was a signal to the ego of impending danger. Not only was there a lack of structure and guidelines but, even worse, there were repeated demonstrations by the children of unpredictable, uncontrollable aggression. The only precedent that could influence him further in his reaction was his experience of some ten years before when he had voluntarily sought to gain experience with disturbed children.

The danger confronting him unconsciously was that he would be rendered helpless and then be subject to his own uncontrollable rage. His past history suggested that he had long feared abandonment and had mastered helplessness by the prompt assumption of some kind of activity. His experience in the classroom was, for him, being abandoned without instructions and feeling that there was nothing he could do. Not only were the children out of control, but perhaps he, too, would soon be out of control. An immediate solution for him was to avoid the threatening situation by not returning to the class. Since this part of the work was not essential in respect to his major interest, he could simply drop the class entirely. Sensitively responsive to the expectations of the scholar with whom he was working, he could not simply walk away from it. Still, the mere thought of returning to the class was enough to precipitate an anxiety attack. The next possible solution was for him to seek help.

On the basis of this formulation, a statement could be made about the patient's chronic pain: the kind of secret, persistent feeling about himself that had become elaborated as a guiding fiction to which he subscribed as he grew up and entered his adult life. Thus, the central issue that was formulated and would be proposed to him in the next meeting, unless other data pointed in a different direction, was as follows: "Although you are a big man physically and although you are successful in your work, you have long been plagued by the fear of helplessness if you are left alone."

In our next meeting, Mr. T spelled out three options open to him. He could just go back to the classroom and sweat it out. Or he could work on it with me; there was simply not enough time for any kind of long-term psychotherapy. Or he could "bag it," that is, he could continue with his particular research and stay away from work with disturbed children.

MR. T: I've been thinking about our meeting last week and I really don't think that the fear of being alone was very prominent in my life. *(I had touched on his fear of being alone and now he was objecting. On the basis of the data, I recognized that his statement was defensive and that inquiry into his objection would be necessary. Perhaps he had had experiences of being alone that should be explored.)*

DOCTOR: Let's look into that . . . were you ever away from home prior to going off to college?

MR. T: Oh, yes. . . I went to camp from age eight to seventeen . . . first as a camper and then as a counselor.

DOCTOR: Tell me what you remember about camp.

MR. T: That's funny . . . all I can remember is going to the railroad station and then getting off at the town nearest the camp.
(I regard this last statement as corroboration for him and for me that going to camp was indeed a struggle for him.)

A treatment proposal was then offered. The central issue as stated above, the work to be done in treatment, was presented. He was offered twelve meetings of forty-five minutes each and a schedule was outlined. Since Mr. T's stay in the area was limited, I offered to meet him once each week for the first eight meetings and twice a week after that in order to complete the work before he left. I set a termination date and asked Mr. T whether he had any questions and for his agreement to the proposal. He had no questions and agreed to the plan. Since we still had some time, I reminded him that this was the first of the twelve meetings.

Additional points reinforcing the central issue promptly emerged. At his home base, he had been working alone in his particular area of interest for about three years when a woman interested in the same area joined the faculty. Whatever loneliness he had felt before was quickly dispelled. More than that, she became involved in his family life. When he gave every evidence of desiring a still closer relationship with her, she demurred and suggested that they had best remain friends. For a week thereafter, he was depressed, and he added, "I never allow depression." He felt that she had abandoned him and described feeling "like a man on crutches whose crutches are broken." A more apt description of helplessness would be difficult to pose.

Very shortly after his marriage, his wife remarked to him that she had been wondering whether it might have been a mistake for them to marry. He was unable to sleep that night for fear that she would leave him.

When Mr. T listens to a lecturer who pauses for ten seconds or so, that pause seems very much longer to him. He becomes restless, fidgets, and feels embarrassed.

DOCTOR: Can you tell me more about what it's like when the pause comes?

MR. T: Well, I begin to wonder whether the lecturer has gotten stuck. Then I become embarrassed for him . . . as if it were I who were up there and stuck . . . I can appreciate that, so then I become somewhat anxious until he starts up again.

DOCTOR: You mean that the pause suggests that the lecturer doesn't know where to go . . . perhaps lost the structure of his lecture . . .

MR. T: I cannot stand empty time . . . I have to be doing something and I have to know what I am doing.

At the end of the meeting, Mr. T asked what we were going to do about the classroom issue. I told him that at some point during the treatment it would be necessary for him to face it.

In our second meeting, Mr. T somewhat sheepishly told me that he had been avoiding the literary collaborator with whom he had been negotiating. He did not want that man to know that he was "bagging out" on the classroom. Moreover, he felt that the man was not living up to the contract that they had agreed on, but he was afraid to voice his discontent lest Mr. R simply tear up the contract. With this kind of information, it was possible to begin to help Mr. T appreciate the extent to which his feelings about himself effectively restricted him from approaching Mr. R, a man whom he recognized as most reasonable.

Mr. T described some of the work he is doing with the scholar who attracted him for his study. Mr. Z is his "guru" and his admiration and respect for Mr. Z are evident. He and Mr. Z share a car pool; on the evening before our meeting, Mr. Z had failed to show up at the expected time to pick up Mr. T for the trip home. Mr. T became very anxious waiting for Mr. Z.

> *(This statement not only indicated the signal anxiety in Mr. T but was also a signal to me, since I could immediately surmise that he had reacted to the fear of being abandoned.)*

DOCTOR: Tell me what the feeling was like as you waited for him.

MR. T: We car pool . . . he's always on time . . . I felt as though I had been left . . . or that he had forgotten . . .

DOCTOR: And then . . .

MR. T: I could have called my wife to come to get me . . .

DOCTOR: Or you could have taken public transportation.

MR. T: No . . . I wouldn't do that . . . I would have to make two changes . . .

DOCTOR: Afraid that you would get lost?

MR. T: I suppose that's why I don't like to ride on the MTA [public transportation] . . . as it turned out, Mr. Z did show up and we drove home.

I reviewed the previous information that we had gathered in respect to his fear of being left alone and the kind of reaction that ensues. He recalled how helpless he felt when he was unable to stop his mother from going off to work and once more, to his own amazement, he realized that he had no recollection of anything about being in camp until he was about age 14 or 15.

As he was leaving the office, he inquired about the shortest route to a particular highway and, after I gave him the information, he properly reminded me that I should have said to him that unless he asks he might fear becoming lost.

The third meeting was mostly devoted to the problem of the classroom. He is troubled about the attitude of the other teachers in that classroom who may recognize that he is "goofing off." Most of all he fears what must be done when one of the children becomes uncontrollable.

> (*Structure and lack of structure, control and lack of control, are central in the patient's personality structure, and whenever he refers to these topics, directly or indirectly, it is imperative that attention be directed to them.*)

DOCTOR: Tell me what happens when one of the kids becomes uncontrollable.

MR. T: Well, he must be removed physically into a quiet room . . .

DOCTOR: What is the quiet room like?

MR. T: It's a padded room, no furniture . . . there is a small screen in the door . . . his belt is taken off . . . and he is left alone.

DOCTOR: And you know something about what it feels like to be left alone.

MR. T: Do you think it's that that gets at me?

DOCTOR: What did you do when you were left alone?

MR. T: I would try to get them not to leave me . . . I would ask them . . . sometimes I would tell them that my tummy hurt . . .

DOCTOR: Did you ever become angry at them?

MR. T: No . . . I never raged at them or threw things or kicked or spit. (*This is the description, of course, of the uncontrollable children in the classroom.*)

DOCTOR: The most you could do was to complain that your belly hurt?

MR. T: Yes, but it didn't work.

DOCTOR: It seems to me that the knot that you have described as coming on in your belly when you are in the classroom is the same knot that you felt when your mother left you in the morning.

MR. T: You mean my body remembers?

At the end of the meeting, Mr. T suggests he would like to see me once more before he tries going to the classroom. I agree.

As we began the fourth session, he told me that he had met with Mr. R and that all his fears had been groundless. Mr. R was clearly unconcerned about whether he went to the classroom, and the writing contract was quickly and amicably settled. On the other hand, Mr. T had felt "all shook up" since our last meeting. He found himself mulling over the image of the child in the quiet room and was aware of his projection, of seeing himself in that child. I reviewed for him how he had experienced the same kind of anxiety a decade earlier in his brief attempt to work with disturbed children, even though those earlier children had not been suffering from impulse disorders. The important point, therefore, was his fear that in any case a child *might* lose control.

> (*And again the subject of control, the meaning of control or loss of control, is to be scanned further. The central issue has now been enlarged and more clearly defined. Thus:*)

DOCTOR: You become so badly frightened not only when a child loses control in reality but even when you think it might happen. Obviously, the element of control, of self-control, is a very touchy one for you . . . tell me about that . . .

MR. T: You know . . . I have always been afraid that I might lose control and that I might never come out of it.

DOCTOR: What do you mean . . . never come out of it?

MR. T: Go crazy . . . yet, something just hit me . . . there was a time when I deliberately challenged control. In my third year at college, I drove two friends to the big city, stopping at every bar en route . . . another time I sky-dived when I was drunk . . .

DOCTOR: Do you recall any such challenge even earlier?

MR. T: When I was seventeen I raced a car at a track . . . I hit a tree and broke my neck . . .

DOCTOR: Have you felt any more of this kind of challenge since college?

MR. T: No, not at all . . . the only way I sometimes imagine myself losing control these days . . . well, I come home and find a man raping my wife and I kill him.

(Mr. T has now given a more graphic picture of his attempts to break through the restraints of control, risking his life in the process. It is important to note that these attempts took place in his adolescence, a time when renewed efforts are made to master earlier conflicts. That he tried desperately bespeaks a degree of ego strength and a capacity for change, since an easier solution for him would have been not to struggle but rather to remain passive and restricted.)

We continued with the question of his anger and how he could not allow its expression when he was a child out of his fear about the meaning of anger. He remembered an incident that occurred in nursery school, when he was 3 years old. His glasses were thrown off his face in a sand fight. His vision was further limited by the sand that had gotten into his eyes. He cried in utter fury, and then his mother appeared and took him home. At age 8, he and a little girlfriend were tossing rocks up in the air. One rock hit her on the head and she bled. He fled in terror, convinced that he had killed her.

(The intimate relationship between fear of helplessness, terrifying rage, and loss of control has been increasingly clarified. He now knows something of his fear about what his anger could do to others and of his resultant fear of retribution, or being abandoned.)

In our fifth session, he promptly told me that he had not yet been able to arrange for his return to the classroom but would do so during this week.

(Resistance was clear enough. However, I made no attempt to pressure him into returning. He knew he would have to do it before very many more of the treatment sessions took place.)

Mr. T was feeling jittery and depressed in this meeting and could not account for it. I asked him to talk about his present state, and he soon realized that today was his birthday. This awareness of growing older reminded him that just three years previously he had had a vasectomy. In the preparation room, before surgery, there had been lying a policeman who was also awaiting a vasectomy. As the policeman was wheeled to the operating room, he suddenly screamed, "Don't let them cut my balls off!" Mr. T was badly shaken and asked to be given a general, rather than a local, anesthetic. Later, his father said that Mr. T was stupid "to have his balls cut off," and this remark was followed by a week-long depression.

(We were witnessing an anniversary reaction that would probably have been manifested in countless depressions had he not been in treatment. The symbolic castration, with its accompanying feelings of loss of masculinity and especially of helplessness, quickly emerged into consciousness in the course of the interview as a logical extension of the work we had been doing. This sophisticated patient was fully aware intellectually of the castration anxiety aroused by the idea of vasectomy and then reinforced by the traumatic incident that occurred. Emotionally, castration anxiety is neither experienced nor recognized in literal terms. Rather, the person becomes aware of the anxious feelings attached to a sense of incompleteness, or inadequacy, or helplessness. To have explored the patient's feelings in terms of his reaction to castration would have yielded only an intellectualized, affectless, consciously meaningless exchange. It was discussed, instead, in terms of the central issue, where it properly belonged.)

Mr. T then associated to his need for perfection as a means both of assuring himself of his intactness and of gaining approval. To make nine A's and one B in high school meant to him that he was "a loser." To be a loser meant that he had failed to live up to the expectations of others and could suffer the loss of their approval. In turn, we were able to clarify how his fear of being left alone meant for him that he was bad, and how he then sought approval, and continues to do so, in order to gain evidence of his goodness.

(A child who seeks a reason for being left alone invariably concludes that there must be something undesirable about him. This kind of statement about oneself serves to maintain the repressive forces that render unconscious the intense rage that is present. The rage is so terribly frightening, in the fantasied destruction it could achieve and in the equally frightening retribution it would summon, that it can be mastered only by its extreme opposite; that is, the total denial of anger and the constant effort to do good so that one will be recognized as a good person.)

Mr. T began the seventh meeting by informing me that he had not made arrangements to return to the classroom but that he had a good "rationalization" for it. He had been appointed to an important panel by Mr. Z and was very anxious to perform well and not make any mistakes, for fear of losing Mr. Z's esteem.

(I felt that more aggressive attention must now be turned to the question of the classroom and his return to it. We had now passed the midpoint of the treatment and soon heightened resistance to termination, another abandonment, would increase his anxiety and harden his resistance to returning to the classroom.)

DOCTOR: Tell me more about your feelings for Mr. Z.

MR. T: You remember that I said he was my guru . . . he is really a wonderful man.

DOCTOR: How else do you feel about him?

MR. T: I have a lot of respect for him . . . I really feel as though he is like a father to me.

DOCTOR: Then, of course, he would be someone whose approval would be crucial to you?

MR. T: Absolutely. You know I always felt that my father cared but he never showed it . . . we're closer now than we've ever been . . . I feel that closeness with Mr. Z and I can't afford to do anything to fail him.

DOCTOR: Then the appointment to the panel means once more that you dare not allow nine A's and one B.

MR. T: It has to be straight A's.

DOCTOR: So again, we see your need to be perfect as the only possible way for you to feel that you are approved, wanted, desirable . . . and since perfection of the kind you seek and need is impossible, there is a built-in guarantee of failure. In fact, your feeling about yourself is that you are a boy among the men.

Mr. T agreed with this statement, and we reviewed his fears about the classroom in terms of his fear of lack of structure, of unpredictable loss of control, of abandonment, and additionally, his fear of failure and the disapproval that would follow. The example of Mr. Z and the panel added further evidence to the predetermined nature of his expectations and responses. I reminded him that the return to the classroom had better be done before we ran out of time in the treatment. He said that he would do it before the next session.

(The phobic situation must be confronted regardless of the kind of treatment. In this interview a degree of pressure was exerted since I recognized that his need for my approval was important to him. Would he fail me and risk my disapproval?)

At the seventh meeting, he reported that he had gone back to the classroom the day before. He had felt some tension but there had not been any "belly knots."

DOCTOR: Tell me what happened.

MR. T: I felt that I handled the kids pretty well . . . the only time that I really felt tense was when we had to place an out-of-control kid in the seclusion room.

DOCTOR: What was that like?

MR. T: Another teacher and I took the kid and we literally had to stuff him into the room.

DOCTOR: You stuffed him into the room . . . like in a box . . . you were very aggressive.

MR. T: I was . . . but I felt good about it . . . I stayed in the class for about three hours and when I left I got rid of it all by busying myself with my other work. As a matter of fact, I had no further thoughts about it until I was on my way here.

He went on to suggest, and I agreed, that he must go back several more times. The discussion then turned again to the pervasiveness of his need to be accepted. He has applied for a particular grant; if it is not funded, then he is a loser. If he fails to receive a top promotion within a year, he is again a loser. He has to be better than anyone else in order to be accepted.

MR. T: I think that I have made pretty good progress here . . . do you think that I will need another *five years* of treatment back at my home base?

DOCTOR: How many sessions do we have left?

MR. T: I don't know . . . four?

DOCTOR: No, five more and not five years. Do you recall the problem that I said you and I would work on?

MR. T: Not at all . . . no recollection.

DOCTOR: It was how you feel helpless when you're left alone . . . and now you are concerned as to how you will manage when I leave you.

MR. T: Oh, yes . . . I remember it now.

(It was not surprising that Mr. T indirectly raised the shadow of termination after the sixth meeting. The seventh meeting is one distinct step beyond the midpoint. It is not unlike the experience of being on a two-week vacation: the first week is usually one of total anticipation of pleasure; the beginning of the second week forces the intrusion of the beginning of the end. In the case of Mr. T, his obsessional adherence to structure and to time would go along with a steady alertness to time: how much time had passed and how much time was left. In ordinary circumstances, this sense of time would be conscious and he would respond to it accordingly. In the treatment situation, his anxiety about the end of our time and his subsequent aloneness forced him into a defensive position of denial. Nevertheless, the pressure of his anxiety was not to be thwarted, so he found himself speaking of the progress he had made [and progress must lead to a conclusion] and then wondering whether he would need five more years of treatment back home. This latter statement clearly indicated his feeling that twelve sessions would not be enough, that he needs more.)

In the eighth meeting, he said he had had a "strange week." Mr. Z had left for a two-week conference. While away, Mr. Z was to review a paper that the two of them had been working on and return it to Mr. T for reworking. However, there had been no word from Mr. Z, and Mr. T was irritated and annoyed. The irritation not only stemmed from the realistic distress over a promise unfulfilled in respect to an important piece of work, but more important emotionally, it had to do with being "left" by Mr. Z for so long a time. Thereupon we again discussed his ever-present problem with separations. I reminded him of his anxiety about "dead time."

MR. T: Dead time reminds me of something else . . . whenever I go to a conference without my wife I will stay up most of the night to avoid going to bed alone.

DOCTOR: You mean that you will keep busy with friends and colleagues until it is no longer possible to avoid going to bed?

MR. T: That's right . . . also, whenever I meet a new person and feel that I resonate with him, I feel that I must let the other person know all about me as quickly as possible . . . then I can read the signals and learn immediately about the future of our relationship.

DOCTOR: You mean that you expose yourself in certain ways sufficient to be able to watch the reaction of the person and know right there whether he accepts you or not.

MR. T: Yes . . . I didn't realize what I was really up to until now . . . it is so important to me to be accepted.

DOCTOR: And to feel wanted.

MR. T: I should tell you of a dream that I had . . . in it Mr. Z offers me a job with him and I grab it . . . I sell my house back home and I come here . . . and then Mr. Z takes a job elsewhere and leaves. (*This is a transparent, almost childlike dream. He has found the people he wants to be wanted by and who appear to want him, Mr. Z and the therapist, but his joy will soon turn to despair. I related the feelings in the dream to his childhood experiences as they continue for him even today. I added that we would keep an eye on his reactions now that the time for him to leave Mr. Z and his institution was only two weeks away. All the data relate to the impending termination of treatment as well. At this point, however, I chose to center the problem on his leaving Mr. Z rather than me. It would be easier for him to do this; we would learn more about the problem of separation and would still have time to bring it back into the treatment as a matter concerning his relationship to me.*)

Today it was almost as an afterthought that he told me that he had gone again to the classroom. Everything was reasonably quiet there and he had felt fine. He intends to continue to go to the classroom.

It is the ninth session and he is aware of strange feelings. He has begun to think it has to do with separation from Mr. Z. He is working twelve to fifteen hours each day, so perhaps it is nothing more than fatigue. He has a further thought about his strange feelings, that perhaps he is trying to develop "a psychological bellyache" in order not to leave Mr. Z.

(*This is an interesting projection. As a child, he sometimes complained of a bellyache in order to get his mother to stay at home with him. Now it is as though Mr. Z, as his parent, should understand that he has a bellyache. The perception of himself as a child in the light of his past experience overtakes his appreciation of the reality of the situation.*)

He knows that he will have to leave Mr. Z, but he doesn't like it. Then he adds that he has recently read something about transference and wonders if these feelings have something to do with me.

(*Since he made the transition to me himself, I suggested that his feelings* do *have to do with me, but that he has been experiencing them mostly in relation to Mr. Z.*)

He is aware that he feels driven in his work now, and I remind him of how he uses activity to avoid certain feelings.

MR. T: I'm going to ask you again . . . will everything fall apart again when I go back home?

DOCTOR: I don't think that you will lose any of your gains . . . more than that, you are addressing a plea to me not to let you go.

MR. T: I guess that's it . . . I think I'm ready to look at my feelings about leaving.

DOCTOR: You and I have come to learn about the many different ways that you have been programmed to react to separation as a result of our work together, and we will have to deal with those feelings in the time that is left before we finish on Friday, July 12.

I suggested further that since he is more sensitive now, it is especially important that he continue to go to the classroom. He agrees but worries about what will happen if he lets all his feelings "hang out" in the classroom. I reminded him of his inclination to think in extremes—nothing hangs out or everything hangs out—and that it need be neither. Before he left, he reviewed with me the dates of our upcoming final three meetings.

As he enters the office for the tenth session, he asks me for a prescription for sleeping pills, indicating that he has a painful back.

DOCTOR: Let's talk about it.

MR. T: I slipped handling my boat on Sunday and fell on my coccyx . . . it hurt and I immediately remembered the pain that I had had when I had multiple surgery for a pilonidal cyst . . . the pain keeps me from sleeping.

DOCTOR: A sleeping pill has no effect on pain.

MR. T: From past experience I know that it works for me . . . I would like a ten-day supply.

(*A* ten-day supply *would bring him precisely to the day of our final meeting.*)

DOCTOR: Suppose I say no.

MR. T: I'll be angry . . . gee, I'm surprised I said that . . . it came right out . . . if you don't give me the prescription it will mean you don't give a damn . . . I could go to the infirmary and get it, but why should I pay twelve bucks for a prescription when you can give it to me.

DOCTOR: You are asking me for succor . . . it is your indirect way of responding to my leaving you . . . if I say no, you become angry and it
means I don't care . . . yet you are asking me for a ten-day supply
. . . exactly to the day that you leave me.

MR. T: Last week, when I raised the question of transference and you said
that I did have such feelings about you . . . when I was driving away
from here I found myself saying, that big shot is crazy . . . and then,
maybe he knows what he is talking about . . .

DOCTOR: What are your feelings about me?

MR. T: Mixed and strange . . . I know I'm angry . . . I say to myself, what
has this guy done for me? . . . What have I gotten for the bucks I
pay? . . . I'll be glad to save the money . . . then I think that I've
learned a lot about myself that I never knew before.

DOCTOR: Do you think that you will miss me?

MR. T: Well, I know we have an agreement that said it would end on a
certain date . . . but I did not at that time expect to feel this way.

I emphasized again the connection between his feelings about my leaving him and his earliest experiences. I told him further that, now that he
knows why he asked me for sleeping pills and his feeling if I should
refuse, I would give him a prescription for five capsules, rather than ten,
because (1) ten would take him to the last day of treatment, and (2) I did
not know what his medical status was.

MR. T: You mean that if it doesn't get better in five nights I should go to the
health service?

DOCTOR: Yes.

In the course of this interview, he also revealed that he had been
engaging Mr. Z more and more in his personal family life in his effort to
hold onto him. He had gone to the classroom yesterday and all went well.
He was tense but otherwise O.K. He had almost wished that one of the
kids would have a blowup so that he could see how he would respond. I
again encouraged him to continue to visit the classroom during this time
of special vulnerability.

*(It may be noted that at times I tell him that I am leaving him and at other times that
he is leaving me. The reality, of course, is that he is the one who is leaving. However,
the intensity of the termination experience is such that the patient invariably experiences, feels, and believes that it is he who is being left, just as it happened in childhood.
Intellectually, the adult in him knows that it is he who is leaving according to
agreement. Emotionally, the feeling is wholly of the past. The gap between adult
intellectual knowledge and childhood perception and feeling should not be underestimated.)*

The eleventh session began with his telling me that his back was better
and that he had used only two pills.

*(The element of winning my approval was undoubtedly again present. However, the
fact is that his back is all right and we will go further into his need for my approval.)*

He had gone to the classroom today both to work and to say good-bye to the people there. He could not have gone there to say good-bye to anyone had he not returned to the classroom. He is feeling very much in control of things. His work will be finished this evening, and on Friday (our last meeting) he and his family will pack up and leave on a shore vacation before returning home. Again he wonders whether he might go back into therapy when he is home.

DOCTOR: We've heard this before . . . you've been telling me that things are in control, so this is your way of saying that you do not wish to separate, to be left, that you want more.

MR. T: I see that . . . but will things fall apart when I am back home?

DOCTOR: I know that you do not wish to leave but I believe that you will do very well.

MR. T: I do feel together . . . I don't feel so tied to Mr. Z and I feel that I will leave him with his respect but without pats on the head . . . like the little boy looking for approval.

He is aware that he wants my approval and that he does have to deal with separating from me. I spoke with him about how, when he was left as a little boy, he could only conclude that he was bad, and to counteract the "badness," he was always looking for approval. Further, if I leave him it means that he is bad.

MR. T: I have thoughts again about winners and losers . . . I came to Boston with four goals to be met in seven months . . . I've done three of them . . . the other is uncertain and will have to wait for some months . . . it has never happened before that I could feel good about batting .750 and not 1.000.

DOCTOR: You remember that nine A's were wiped out by one B . . . you have sought for perfection in order to be approved, admired, wanted, and that desire could never be met or satisfied because you would simply have to make ten A's every day.

MR. T: I've never been able to settle for less . . . I marvel at my contented reaction . . . I've really come to feel very differently about myself over the few months here . . . I didn't realize when I started what kind of intensity would be created by the time limit and how strongly I would feel about the end . . . well, now I have only to deal with leaving you at our last session.

At our twelfth and final meeting he is feeling "high." His work is all done and he was able to sit at his desk and read two books this morning.

(*My suspicion is aroused. Is the "high" that he is feeling evidence of an inability to manage the separation? Is he moving into activity as a means of avoiding feelings that might merge into pathological overactivity?*)

DOCTOR: You read two books this morning?

MR. T: I read that way . . . it was not a driven feeling . . . I felt relaxed and I was able to reflect on how many aspects of my professional work have come together in a way that I've never been able to do before.

DOCTOR: How else have you been feeling?

MR. T: Last night my wife and I had dinner with Mr. Z. . . . then we went home and I watched TV . . . something I rarely do . . . I slept "like a rock" all night and that's not too usual for me either.

DOCTOR: More?

MR. T: I'm aware that maybe I'm warding off other feelings but I do feel that rather than this being only a termination . . . for me it is a beginning . . . a new world of options has been opened to me that I never knew before.

DOCTOR: I agree with you . . . nevertheless, you might be avoiding other feelings . . . you may feel depressed or angry in the next days and if you do it will have to do with feelings about me.

MR. T: I realize that your approval of me has become important.

I used this remark to tell him that he has always sought approval, but since I am not in any position to promote him, give him references, or otherwise help his career, his feeling must be based on an old state of affairs. His wish for my approval is really the old wish for parental approval.

DOCTOR: Do you like me?

MR. T: I really do.

DOCTOR: Then you may feel that since you worked so hard for me, why do I send you away, why do I leave you.

MR. T: I know that I have made great gains and I know, too, about the gap between my head and my gut . . . of course, you may have had better patients.

DOCTOR: Shall I give you an A or A plus?

MR. T: I'm really satisfied with .750 . . .

DOCTOR: But you see that there is the hint again of your wish for my approval.

MR. T: You know, I've had the feeling of instant cure . . . I'm suspicious of that . . . in thirteen sessions.

(He has all along counted the initial evaluation interview as one, hence thirteen.)

DOCTOR: You are not cured . . . you will run up against these problems again, but you will know what they are about and be able to handle them.

MR. T: The compression of time is strange . . . what seemed so far in the future when we started is now about over.

DOCTOR: I warn you again that you may feel depressed, or angry, or both, and it will have to do with feelings about me.

MR. T: I think I'm in control . . . I feel that way . . . and I'll handle it.

And we say good-bye.

(The above is obviously not a verbatim report of the entire session, but the highlights are presented. I do wish to make the point that in all the sessions, and especially the last one, the therapist does not sit back and wait for the patient to come himself to near or full clarity about particular issues. There is no time for that. However, this method of treatment does facilitate the patient's associations and recall so well that enough information is gained to allow the therapist confidence in his reconstruction of the

central issue for the use of the patient. The time limit and the intense transference that it stimulates allow for the detailed elaboration of the central issue as well as for its resolution. Thus, in this last session, it is likely that I was as active as the patient in the dialogue exchange.)

Follow-up eight months later

Eight months after Mr. T returned to his home, which was distant from Boston, I wrote to him. At the time treatment ended he had had no inkling that I had any intention of making contact with him again. As is my custom, I told him that a period of time has elapsed and I was interested to know how things had gone for him. Rather than asking him any questions, I left it to him to tell me as much or as little as he chose of his feelings about our work together.

Below are excerpts from Mr. T's long letter, which was accompanied by a copy of the paper that he had written with Mr. Z during his leave.

> I was very pleased to get your recent note. Somehow, the eight months since we last met seem to have passed more rapidly than most other eight-month periods in my life. Of course, I still remember both cognitively and affectively, in my head and my gut, many of our interactions. The joint result of these interactions has made life a little easier and has made my attitudes and feelings about a number of domains of my own personal existence more coherent. . . .

He then goes into considerable detail about his work, with its multiple responsibilities and frustrations. He continues:

> Given this background of intense frustration and lack of time to do any serious thinking, my head is in surprisingly good shape.

He reviews the three goals that he set for himself on his leave: (1) the paper that he wrote with Mr. Z has been widely accepted and highly praised; (2) the possibility of getting his grant funded remains uncertain; and (3) his aim of achieving a promotion to top status before he reaches the age of 35 seems highly probable. He adds a fourth goal this time—closeness with his family—and he feels that he and his family are very much "together."

> Now if you consider these domains as four "times at bat," that means I'm batting .500 for sure, with the possibility of batting .750 or 1.000. As we discussed, and as I now honestly believe, batting .500 in the majors is pretty good.
>
> In a funny kind of way, I'm more acutely aware of the problem of feeling alone than I was before, even though I'm better able to deal with it and see how it becomes manifest in various situations. Being or feeling alone is still a

problem. I am more aware that it is the root cause of a number of insecurities and "minidepressions" that I feel and live through. Surprisingly, I am not aware of "missing you"; I am aware of missing Mr. Z but that missing does not hurt . . . although I know and feel that our work together was most productive, I will be in a better position to assess the extent to which I *know* that I can "make it" on my own a year or so from now.

In closing, let me say that just as Mr. Z facilitated my cognitive development, so I believe and feel that you facilitated my affective development. I thank you very deeply for this.

6

Severe Hypochondriacal Reaction: *(Giving Doesn't Mean Deserving)*

Mrs. T is a 40-year-old married woman with four children ranging in age from 5 to 14. She immediately explained that she had come for help because of severe hypochondriacal symptoms that she had had for at least a decade and that had worsened during the preceding two years. (She did not use the term "hypochondriacal" since she has never been able to accept the possibility that something other than her physical symptoms was at the root of her fears.) She said she did not expect to live long because she believed she had cancer. At this very moment of the interview she felt near panic as she showed me a small adhesive strip on her face. A "pimple" had been removed for biopsy and she would hear the "verdict" later that day. She added that even if she is told that it is an easily treated skin cancer, she will continue to be tormented with the idea that it is only a manifestation of an internal cancer. As might be assumed, there is a long history of innumerable visits to physicians for checkups and for reassurance. Nevertheless, she began to cry as she related her conviction that she did not have long to live.

She is unable to watch television if the program involves cancer. She often sleeps poorly and eats compulsively when depressed. Several years earlier, when an acquaintance had died of cancer, the patient had suffered from the same symptoms she had seen in her friend and had been unable to eat. Shortly after the birth of her second child, she and her husband had gone on a brief vacation, leaving the two children with her mother-in-law, with whom there had been considerable friction. On returning home, she developed a headache that continued without relief for one whole year.

After receiving negative medical and neurological test results, she accepted referral to a psychiatrist. This had been about ten years ago. She saw the psychiatrist for a year, at which point she decided to stop treatment because she felt she had made "some gains" and saw no need to continue. Four years before the present interview, she had seen another psychiatrist because of chronic belly pain, but had again stopped after one and a half years, feeling that she had learned to assert herself with others and manage her life better. She never felt free of symptoms, however, and when a new set of symptoms appeared about four months ago, she consulted a psychiatrist, who referred her to me. The new symptoms consisted of burning sensations in her arms and legs, accompanied by severe anxiety.

The patient had been born and raised in this area and had gone to local public schools. In this preliminary interview, she reported that she had been trained as a highly specialized medical technician; she was currently working in the hospital where her father had died of a coronary at the age of 48. She never could remember the month of his death until a recent conversation with her sister. She had been deeply attached to her father and had worried about his hypertension. She recalled that she had often listened for his loud snoring at night to be certain that he was still alive. Mother is alive and well and lives alone. Although she described mother as very independent, the patient has always felt responsible for her and said that she felt that she had been a mother to her mother. Here she remarked that she is aware of her compulsion to assume responsibility, which then becomes a burden to her. She has two younger sisters.

The patient has been married for thirteen years to an able, active man who is a good provider and is generally supportive and sympathetic toward her. For the past three years, she has been taking a mild antianxiety medication, which was prescribed by her favorite internist shortly before he moved to another part of the country. She still mourns his departure. She continued with another internist, who retired recently; again, she felt the loss keenly. She is now seeing a third internist.

As she described her behavior with her children and her mother, and in her social and charitable activities, it became evident that she was an obsessive-compulsive character with an overwhelming, compulsive need to "do for" others. She agreed with my suggestion that this need was accompanied by an inner feeling that she was undeserving.

(Her compulsion to do for others, along with her persistent feeling of unworthiness, suggested that her anticipation of early death was the result of an unconscious expectation of punishment.)

Her earliest memory went back to some point before the age of 5. She is in a store with her parents; they leave and she suddenly finds herself alone—abandoned—and becomes panicky. She has never been certain whether this was a dream or a real event; when she told her parents about it, they had no recollection of it. For Mrs. T, it is a recurrent and very vivid image.

(I raised the question to myself whether this memory of abandonment might have coincided with the birth of her next younger sister.)

During the interview, the patient often cried. She presented herself in an overserious way, as though intent on convincing me of her need for help. I remarked that she seemed to feel terribly undeserving and condemned to die and that understanding why she felt that way was very important.

MRS. T: Do you think I can be helped?
DOCTOR: Yes, but there is further information that I would like to have, and then I will suggest what we might do.

She agreed to this.

In the second interview, further details of her past history corroborated my first impressions of her problem. It seemed to me that she was a compulsive do-gooder who must feel undeserving, because she becomes furious with her need to be good and to give of herself constantly, with little gratifying return or recognition. Her anger must be tied, I felt, to sadistic, guilt-provoking fantasies that increase her sense of unworthiness, which in turn increases her need to be good and to do for others. In addition, if she is not good, she will be abandoned and unloved. Again anger returns, mobilizing guilt, which is mastered by further "do-gooding." Thus, she is trapped in this sequence of affects.

The question might be raised whether all these impressions could be substantiated in the course of one full interview and part of a second. The answer lies in two important sources of data: first, the information provided directly by the patient; and second, the fact that an accurate diagnosis of the patient's psychological state allows certain generalizations about the patient's problems. That is to say that the diagnosis of obsessive-compulsive character, with the variety of somatic symptoms presented by the patient, does allow for an understanding of the dynamic interplay of facts and affects and consequences that holds true for all patients so diagnosed. Details will vary from one person to another, but the human responses and attempts at mastery will differ only in their intensity, which in turn determines the extent to which the underlying conflicts interfere with gaining reasonable gratification in everyday life. In this instance, the patient had sought to master her chronic pain by persistent efforts to convince others of her worthwhileness. The long history of hypochondriacal concerns pointed both to the unconscious need for the attention and loving concern of others and to the continuing failure of her adaptive mode. It might be well to note that the history as presented here includes the essential details; it is not a verbatim record. Presenting it accurately depends on the interviewer's skill in examining the data given by the patient and in discriminating what is most important, less important, and of no discernible importance.

About a third of the way through the second interview, enough data had been gained to warrant presenting the central issue to the patient, to be followed by a treatment proposal.

DOCTOR: You have always given of yourself to so many others and yet you feel and always have felt both undeserving and unrewarded.

MRS. T: You mean by my husband?

DOCTOR: You feel unloved by him and by all others.

MRS. T: I often feel that I have no friends at all . . . in a few months I am taking on a responsible assignment for an organization and already I am thinking about the tension and the sleepless nights and what else will happen.

(Again she is confronting a situation in which she will be called on to give a great deal of herself and again she will have to cope with her contradictory affect, which will give rise to her characteristic somatic response.)

At this point, I offered her the treatment proposal of twelve sessions, ending on a specific date, with the central issue as the subject of our attention. She agreed to go through with it.

She promptly began to speak of her lack of self-confidence. When she was in the sixth grade, she wished to transfer to a very prestigious public school. For reasons unknown to her, her parents were advised that she should not go there. She did poorly on her college boards and was rejected by a local university. Eventually, she did gain admission to an out-of-state university, where she struggled with the work and her lack of confidence. She did not return to college after her freshman year, but instead undertook specialized medical technician training. She excelled in this and soon was teaching others. She gained admission to the local university that had rejected her, earned her bachelor's degree, and went on to win her master's with honors. These achievements had no effect on her lack of self-confidence. At age 25, she married and soon became pregnant. She has been a housewife ever since.

She then thought about her mother and recalled how mother was easily angered and would beat her and her younger sister with a strap. At such times, the two girls would shut themselves in a closet to escape the strap. Sister would often emerge and face up to mother; the patient never could. To this day, a certain tone in her mother's voice recalls the strap for her and she becomes frightened. She tried to be a very good girl and do everything that her mother told her to do. As she was about to leave the first session, she added that the facial lesion had been found to be benign, but that she had been unable to go to the doctor alone to learn the result; she had to have her husband with her.

(*Even in this last bit of information one can see an important dynamic of her problem. The husband must be made to show his concern by coming with her, even though the likelihood of malignancy was remote and the two of them had been through this same kind of visit to doctors many times before.*)

In the second meeting, one week later, she began by saying that she had been very much upset when she left the first session. She had become very angry and was "noncommunicative" with her husband all week until they had gone off for the weekend to relax. There she told him that she was angry with him because he was so unresponsive to her feelings. He remarked that she too was unresponsive. After this exchange, they both felt better. Actually, during the past week she had taken less of her antianxiety medication than usual.

She had checked her memory of mother hitting the children with a strap with her sister, who corroborated her recollections. She was surprised at her sudden awareness that her sister hits her children; the patient never hits hers. She could see the connection between that early painful situation with her mother and her attempt to cope with it by becoming a good girl. She recalled that when she baby-sat for her sisters, every time the parents returned later than expected, she would endure a steadily increasing panic that something had happened to them and they would never come back.

(*Bad enough that she had to endure the presence of younger rivals but, even worse, she had to take care of them. Anger at this charge created fantasies about something happening to her parents, which immediately led to the fear of punishment—that the parents would abandon her for good. This whole turn of events reinforced her need to be good so that the feared punishment would never occur.*)

The patient reported that she had verified with her husband her memory of the time they left their children with the mother-in-law. She confirmed with him that the headache had begun then.

MRS. T: You know, I just remember again that memory or dream, whatever it is, about my parents abandoning me in the store.

DOCTOR: You did to your little daughter what was done to you; you felt that you had abandoned her and you became sick.

MRS. T: I never thought of that.

DOCTOR: You have the need to be good out of fear that you will be left, unloved and uncared for.
(*I repeat the central issue to her.*)

MRS. T: I don't think I want to go on with these thoughts about myself . . . I feel a churning inside, my arms and face feel like they are burning.

DOCTOR: You are always ready to feel guilty.

The patient then reported that, when her father died, the young man who was courting her had come to the house on a condolence call. She had gone into her bedroom with him and they had embraced. She later felt awful that she had embraced him at a time of mourning.

MRS. T: If people knew how I feel about myself, how dumb I am . . .

DOCTOR: You assume responsibility for any situation or task with the feeling that you have to live up to what you feel are the expectations of others . . . so much of this is of your own making and with it you come to feel so tense.

(I remind myself after the patient leaves to watch for her tension in respect to living up to what she perceives as my expectations of her. For example, it is likely that she feels that she must do the work of treatment in the ten sessions that are left; she must do it for me rather than for herself.

In the above session and in others to follow, some may feel that the doctor is being too interpretive on the basis of the patient's remarks in the session, or that the interpretations appear to be unrelated to where the patient is at. An effective therapeutic process is one in which the therapist actively associates to the patient's material. In so doing, associative data from earlier remarks of the patient or from earlier sessions are brought to center stage. Thus, intimate connections are brought together from disparate points in the therapeutic process.)

In the third session, she felt apprehensive. She had had a bad week, with a variety of gastrointestinal upsets, much tension, and a good deal of concern whether the pains she was experiencing in her right lower quadrant might be cancer. I directed her attention to our last meeting, when she had turned away and would not continue talking about her fear of being abandoned.

MRS. T: There are times when I am afraid that my husband will leave me. I went to a meeting in which a lot of men were involved and I felt ignored, superfluous, and depressed. I told my husband about it and I cried. He said I was making too much of it.

DOCTOR: You were hurt by the men and then you became angry.

MRS. T: Now that you mention it, I was angry with those men even before the meeting . . . I knew how they would act with me.

DOCTOR: How must a woman feel who always has to please everyone of significance to her?

MRS. T: Frustration.

DOCTOR: Anger.

MRS. T: I suppose I give myself very little credit for anything.

DOCTOR: You are very hard on yourself. For example, you must feel apprehensive and tense here because of what you must feel are my expectations of you with so little time available.

MRS. T: I see that and I know that I am here to do something for myself and not for you . . . but what has all this to do with my symptoms?

DOCTOR: Your symptoms serve to avoid—to keep away from your awareness—your feelings, especially angry feelings.

MRS. T: Why?

DOCTOR: Let's ignore the why of it at this point and see rather how you have come to an automatic way of relating . . . to give and give in the hope of acceptance, and inevitably you come to suffer frustration and anger . . . that is what we should look at further.

MRS. T: What about my fear that I haven't long to live?

DOCTOR: We will have to wait on that . . . I know that this is all very difficult and painful for you.

MRS. T: Do you still think I can be helped?

DOCTOR: Yes.

(These important points of the third session highlight much of what goes on in this patient. There are men in the organization to which she devotes so much of her energy, and they brush her aside. At least, that is how she feels. We use the incident to begin to help her become aware of some feelings aroused in her that are very different from her accustomed awareness of herself as only doing good for others. She is able to respond affirmatively, but she soon falls back on her symptoms to protect her from such feelings. However, we have made a start.)

She began our fourth meeting by telling me that after our last session she had gotten belly pain while at the movies. It had come on when she became aware of the intense father-daughter attachment depicted in the film. Later she had become angry with her husband and, to her surprise, she had not felt her usual desire to make up with him. As a matter of fact, she said, she was pleased for him to stay out of her way altogether; she was pleased to be able to show him that she doesn't need him. She had even gone so far as to make the conscious decision to please herself by going alone to a movie that she was eager to see.

She continued with her story of progress as she told me of visiting a neighbor woman who has cancer and whom the patient had never been able to visit before. This time, she had gotten up her courage and made the visit. She found the woman most courageous and able to talk freely about her rather horrifying symptoms. During this recital, the patient almost panicked. The night before our meeting, she had turned on the television and watched a film about breast cancer. She forced herself to listen and to watch and felt good for having done so. Anyway, she hastily added, she doesn't worry about breast cancer.

(In this fourth interview, the patient is pleased to report her growing sense of freedom. It is not unusual for patients to feel better during this early phase of treatment; in fact, it is a very common response to the positive transference that has been set in motion. The therapist is the good parent who understands and will undo the pain. In this instance, however, an

additional element is introduced, insofar as the patient has an inordinate need to please. One must then consider how much of the patient's progress can be attributed to the need to please, with its accompanying hope that some kind of reward will be forthcoming.)

MRS. T: A friend of mine is going to the hospital for open heart surgery and needs blood. . . . I would like to give but I am afraid that the needle might be dirty or I might even faint. . . .

DOCTOR: Your friend needs blood and you have your fears about that . . . any other reason?

MRS. T: I even called to find out how long it would take to regenerate a pint of blood.

DOCTOR: So you feel caught between your wish to give and your fears about what might happen to you.

MRS. T: I don't know what to do.

DOCTOR: Does it occur to you that one possibility might be that you really do not wish to give at all?

MRS. T: I hadn't thought of that.

DOCTOR: It may well be that you don't want to give, and instead of being honest with yourself, you conceal your reluctance with a host of reasons. I think that this is another instance in which you feel that you give and give but don't recognize the feeling that you don't have enough left in you to do that.

MRS. T: Maybe . .

(If the patient had been asked to give of her time for her friend, she would have had no objections. She is asked to give of her body substance and, in the light of her somatic preoccupations and fear of death, the therapist can readily understand her dilemma. One who is so much aware of her need to give invariably feels drained. The sense of being drained becomes concretized in terms of body substance, which leads to the idea that there is so little left in one's body that one pint of blood could well tip the scales toward disaster.)

We then discussed her panic reactions, and this led her to speak of her fear of death and dying. As a medical technician, she would carefully steer clear of rooms in which there was a dead patient. When her father died in the hospital where she was employed, she could not get herself to go to his room. She told of her attachment to him and how he loved her, how warm, friendly, and full of fun he was. She said that mother "brought me up"; by this she meant that mother laid down all the rules of behavior and was the strict taskmaster. She again recalled her persistent concern about her father's health long before he died.

DOCTOR: We see that death and dying are related all the way back to your concerns about your father. After he died, you became preoccupied with your death and it has continued. We will have to learn more about that.

MRS. T: Should I give blood to my friend? Would that be better for me?

DOCTOR: How did you feel when you made yourself watch the cancer film on television?

(She smiles as though to say she knows she will feel better if she does give blood.)

She begins her fifth visit by telling me what an awful week she has had; it was so bad that she had not felt like coming to see me today. She was at odds with her husband and would not talk with him. In return, he withdrew from her. She felt like "exploding" over the involvement of her husband and children in a new business venture of his from which she felt excluded. At one point during the week, her son had asked her to pick up a tennis ball for him and she promptly blew up at him. She had felt so put upon by everyone that she began to cry, whereupon her husband bawled her out for crying. Angrily, she spoke to him about their separating. He said that he would never leave the house and children and that she could go. She responded that she would not leave either.

(It is not the first time that Mrs. T has been so angry, but it is the first time that she has felt her anger. Characteristic of the person heavily given to obsessional defenses, the tendency to think in extremes promotes the fear that this is the only way in which feelings can be experienced. That is to say, their reactions are all or none. Thus, Mrs. T goes on to say that when her anger subsided and she made up with her husband, she felt relieved of a huge burden: "something was over and done with . . . like dying and death.")

She continues to wonder about her anger as she recalls her father and asks herself whether she was angry with him for placing responsibility for his illness on her. She promptly recognizes that she took the responsibility on herself and could hardly blame father. She is aware now that anger, crying, and depression are common experiences for her.

MRS. T: I did a lot of crying in my previous therapies . . . but not here.
DOCTOR: Can you account for that?
MRS. T: I have to control it here . . . I don't have much time . . . if I cry, it will distract me and I'll lose time . . . I always feel that time is pressing on me.
DOCTOR: Then you must feel that I am placing great pressure on you since you feel you have to fulfill my expectations and I don't give you much time.
MRS. T: That's true . . . I can see that.
DOCTOR: Perhaps you are angry with me.
MRS. T: I'm not aware of it . . . I like you . . . I find you to be a warm person.
(This is a first attempt to bring something of the patient's transference feelings into the open. The patient denies the possibility and no effort is made to press any further at this time.)

As she left, I asked her whether she had been a blood donor last week. With some embarrassment, she said that she had entirely forgotten about it. In fact, she had given blood, had been interested in seeing the new techniques for taking blood, and had been quite pleased with herself. She also told me that she would miss her session next week because she was going on a brief vacation with her husband.

(It would be appropriate to remark here that, in such instances of cancellation, the patient is not penalized. The termination date is simply extended by another week. When cancellations become repetitive, one must deal with the resistance manifested by such behavior. Absences on this latter basis are infrequent in time-limited psychotherapy.)

In the sixth session, she tells me that the one-week vacation with her husband and children was very bad. She resented the presence of the children, felt irritable and moody, and preferred to be alone. Usually, she is extremely apprehensive about a plane flight, but this time she didn't care if anything happened. She had felt unable to relax and was aware of the thought that she would like to have had an affair. She had never allowed such thoughts before.

DOCTOR: You're experiencing a good deal of anger and it must be something that you feel toward me.

MRS. T: I don't see why . . .

DOCTOR: Well, you're feeling a good deal of pressure from me . . . so little time . . .

MRS. T: What will happen to me if I feel no better at the end and you send me on?

DOCTOR: How much time do we have . . . how many sessions left?

MRS. T: I don't know . . .

DOCTOR: Guess . . .

MRS. T: Five . . .

DOCTOR: No, we still have six.

MRS. T: The pressure of time is always there.

DOCTOR: The pressure of time is really the pressure that you feel from people . . . from me . . . the pressure as to whether you can do it here.

MRS. T: It makes me angry . . . I am so much more aware of being angry . . .

(At this point, I reconstructed for her how she came to feel that she was so bad a person: (1) at age 3, she had been left alone on the street by her parents [it seems quite certain that this memory is a screen for the birth of her sister and being left by mother]; (2) her mother had hit her with a strap; (3) she baby-sat for others and panicked about her parents not returning; (4) even when there was no marital conflict, she feared that her husband would leave her. She responded with the recollection of a recurrent dream in which she is not married, is left all alone, and panics.)

DOCTOR: All of this has to do with the sense of your having been left because you were bad and you have been trying desperately ever since to please, to give, to be loved . . . but you can never believe it when you do have it. You have never been able to feel yourself to be an acceptable human being who deserves to live. When your doctor

says that you are O.K., you can only believe it temporarily.
(*Mrs. T cries.*)

DOCTOR: Can you believe that you are an acceptable human being who deserves to live?

MRS. T: I'll try.

(*It is apparent that treatment has mobilized much of the patient's deeply
warded-off anger that has followed on her almost lifelong feeling of being
victimized by just about everyone with whom she has had more than
casual contact. Her chronic pain has been graphically brought to light
and its multiple sources revealed. The time limit is experienced by the
patient as an almost intolerable source of pressure. Even as she is helped to
recognize and experience the old roots of her present distress, she cannot
help also responding to the time limit as typical of the ever-present demands on her to fulfill the needs and expectations of others—in this instance, of the therapist.*)

The extent to which the patient responds to the time limit is again
revealed when she comes for the seventh meeting. She says how bad she
feels, but what can she expect with only three sessions left? Surely, there
was no chance that she could feel better.

(*It is not at all clear how she had misinterpreted the treatment proposal to include only
ten sessions. A likely possibility is that the distortion was generated by her angry
feeling that she was giving so much in this treatment and getting so little.*)

She went on to say that the three people she has the most trouble with
are her husband, his mother, and her own mother. She feels that she
treats her own mother the worst of all. With all three, the same thing is
true, namely, the feeling that demands are being made on her. With
everyone else she manages better, by maintaining some distance from
them. If she allows herself to come too close to others, she fully expects
that she will be abandoned no matter how much she gives. To my query,
she said that she could not remember the question I had raised to her the
week before. (The question was whether she could accept herself as a
decent human being who deserves to live.) I remind her of the question;
she responds that she feels hopeless and despairs that she can ever
change. I suggest to her that, in order to change, she must first wish to
change; then we would have to search further to learn more about what
makes her feel so devalued.

(*I would like to comment on my suggestion that the patient must first wish to change. I
believe that most patients who finally bestir themselves to see a psychiatrist are
genuinely motivated to change. They have had enough distress and are eager for relief.
It is a rare person who can anticipate how painful self-examination may be—often
much more painful over a brief time span than anything experienced before treatment.
As defenses give way under continued self-probing, powerful feelings that were previously defended against begin to emerge with frightening intensity. It is at such points*)

in treatment that the challenge to the patient is greatest, and exclamations of hopelessness are frequent. Concurrently, the desire to flee treatment may offer a way out. It is at such junctures in treatment that the patient may need to be reminded of the wish to change that brought him for help. There is something to be said, too, about mobilizing the patient's will for change, for the patient to make the conscious decision that he does wish to change and wills himself to work toward that end. It is a responsibility that each patient must sooner or later assume in treatment without relying on medication or behavioral manipulations; even the dependence on the therapist must yield to the patient's own desire to effect change.)

The patient continued to speak of her guilt about her behavior in respect to the three people she had said were most trouble for her. In general, she was feeling quite well except for some continuing pain in her right lower quadrant.

(In this seventh session, she clearly is responding to the fact that the treatment is moving toward an end. Her error as to the number of sessions only highlights her feeling about the impending separation. Even if she had remembered the number of sessions correctly, she would have been aware that we were at the halfway mark. It is not uncommon for patients to express their disappointment or their hopelessness about change at the mid-point of treatment. Early anticipations of a rapid "cure"—enhanced by the patient's positive, unambivalent response to the therapist—have been replaced by the return of ambivalence as it was originally experienced with the important early figure[s].)

In the eighth session, Mrs. T looked very well. She had been away with her husband since the last session. She had had a good time and had been very much aware that only when she is away from her usual responsibilities can she feel free of obligations and allow herself full relaxation and pleasure. Nevertheless, she had had one bad scrap with her husband, who she feels always puts her down. She told of having been preoccupied with a word I had used at our last meeting; she simply could not remember what it was. Suddenly, she remembered that I had said she did not feel "deserving"—that was the word—and she agreed that she did feel undeserving. With this kind of feeling, it makes sense that she would need to go all out to please. Again, she thought of how hard it was for her to deal with the three important people in her current life. Her mother is unceasingly critical of her, and she wonders if she unknowingly acts the same way. I pointed out that her mother tends to dump her woes on the patient, who then feels that she is supposed to do something about them. I added that such situations could only provoke her sense of helplessness, which in turn could account for her constant irritation with her mother. The sense of responsibility for mother carried her thoughts to the same kind of feeling about her father and his death. She recalled her father once going to fix a water pipe. She grabbed at his arms to stop him for fear that the effort might affect his heart. He angrily showed her her fingernail marks on his arms where she had clutched him too tightly. That night he suffered his coronary attack.

I reviewed again how certain events in her life had led her to feel that she was a bad and undeserving little girl. She wondered if her selection of a husband was influenced by these feelings about herself. I suggested that we might go into how she and her husband got together. As she left, she remarked that she still did not know how many more sessions there were.

In the ninth meeting, she asks me to tell her, to evaluate for her, what her problems are and how well she is meeting them.

DOCTOR: How many meetings do we have left?

MRS. T: I don't know.

DOCTOR: We have three more after this one and I believe you are worried about what you will do after you leave me.

MRS. T: That's true.

DOCTOR: And you don't want to leave me or for me to let you go.

MRS. T: That's also true.

I decided to postpone more intensive work on termination and so remarked that we would go into further detail about the question of leaving next time. At this point, I felt it would be a good idea to look into the details of how she met and married her husband. Before she met her husband, she had been going with a man for whom she cared a good deal. He returned to his native city and then wrote a letter telling her that she was not intellectual enough for him. She felt enormously put down and hurt but carried on in her usual efficient manner.

Some months later she met her husband. They went together for several years before marrying since he seemed unable to make up his mind. Eventually, she insisted on a decision and they married shortly thereafter. She is aware of all his fine qualities but feels that he is very much like his mother in that he is dogmatic, must always be right, and is verbally abusive. I suggested that, since he was not likely to change, she must not let him erode her self-respect. The session ended after she informed me that she has had minimal physical discomfort for some weeks now.

Mrs. T begins the tenth session with a question:

MRS. T: Did I marry R out of the feeling that I had to have someone who would put me down?

DOCTOR: In view of your relationship with the man who preceded your husband, and in the light of all that we have learned, it is likely that you could not have chosen someone who would have placed you on a pedestal.

MRS. T: You mean this thing about being undeserving?

DOCTOR: Yes.

MRS. T: Then my relationship with my husband can change only by changes that I make myself?

DOCTOR: Yes.

She tells again of her persistent efforts to get her mother-in-law to like her despite endless rebuffs. I remind her of her constant, undiscriminating efforts to please and to be liked. During the previous weekend, she had met a woman her age who had had an eye removed due to a tumor. Soon she began to feel that her vision was impaired and she had a headache over her right eye. She talked herself out of it but worries about not being able to do that after this treatment is over.

At this point, I review the onset of her symptoms in relation to her father's illness, her love for him, and her guilt about his illness. Further, as a result, she had felt an exceptionally strong need to be comforted after she lost him. She begins to cry and tells me how much she is like her father. I remark that her physical symptoms mean that she feels she does not deserve to live. She tearfully agrees that this has been her feeling. I review her feeling of badness and tell her forthrightly that she deserves to live and to be loved. She cries openly now.

DOCTOR: You soon will have to say good-bye to me.

MRS. T: I always hate to say good-bye . . . it's like death . . . I know that we'll be through in two weeks, but what will I do if I need you when this is over?

DOCTOR: You are avoiding saying good-bye. Did you have any trouble saying good-bye to your previous therapist?

MRS. T: No, I decided that we had gone as far as we could . . . and I wasn't attached to them.

DOCTOR: You must feel then that you are attached to me.

MRS. T: No . . . (cries) . . . maybe I am . . . a doctor relative of mine from Peoria visited with us over the weekend . . . he looks like you and talks like you . . . I am very fond of him . . .

DOCTOR: So it will be very difficult for you to say good-bye to me.

Mrs. T smiles, but looks very tearful. Again she asks for an evaluation of her total state and progress. I ask if she means that she wants something comparable to a complete physical examination, and she replies in the affirmative. I remind myself that she wants me to tell her that I approve of her and like her.

(The termination process is in full course now. She is able to admit her feelings but then generally promptly denies them. She is not conscious of this process of admission and denial, even though her associations clearly corroborate my description of her feelings about leaving me. The intensity of her need to deny her feelings, not to face up to them, is sharply revealed in her remark that saying good-bye is like death.)

In the eleventh session, Mrs. T said that she was feeling quite well. Her husband had left on a business trip the day before and, before his departure, they had gotten into a scrap. She had become upset, cried, and left the room without saying good-bye. Later she realized that she had been angry with him for going away and leaving her with all the responsibility for the family. It became clear that she felt good because she had been able herself to recognize what the quarrel had been about. She did not, however, make the connection to the impending separation in treatment.

I brought up termination, and she said that she really felt very well and was without symptoms. She has some mixed feelings about ending but, since she has known about the time limit from the start, she has simply come to accept it. Further, she is not aware of any special feelings toward me. She might have had some if this had been a reciprocal relationship rather than just one of patient and doctor. Knowing the time limit, she has protected herself from getting too involved with me. She then recalled that her mother had always told her *never to tell others of her feelings* or what went on in the family. We talk about her fear of her feelings and I suggested the vulnerability she would encounter if she let herself feel something toward me. Her resistance remained intact until we returned to the question of her deserving to live.

MRS. T: I have always felt that my time is *limited* . . . that I would die young . . . and I still feel that way . . . (she begins to cry) . . . I'm afraid that it will all return after I'm through . . . what will I do?
DOCTOR: You mean then that I should not let you go.
MRS. T: At least if I knew I could come back to see you.
DOCTOR: We will talk some more about that next week.

(*In time-limited psychotherapy, I have been impressed with the minimum amount of acting out, which I ascribe to the structure of the treatment model and the close adherence to the central issue as a means of limiting regression. It is important to watch for acting out in the termination phase, where it is most likely to appear. Such acting out is clearly related to the transference and must be so understood. Thus, Mrs. T has an angry spat with her husband in which she leaves him before he leaves her. In accord with the meaning of acting out, her behavior serves to maintain resistance against the separation from the therapist.*)

In the twelfth and final meeting, she expressed two major concerns. Yesterday and today she has had burning sensations in her skin and is aware that it has to do with anger. She anxiously wonders what she will do if her symptoms return.

DOCTOR: You want me to tell you to stay?
MRS. T: No . . . I only want to know whether I can return if things go wrong.
DOCTOR: You are the kind of person who likes schedules and assurances . . . there are no guarantees in the task of living and you will have to take your chances like the rest of us . . . give yourself some time . . . I think that you will do all right and if you come to feel that you need help, you'll know what to do.

I reviewed what we had learned about her that made sense of her feelings about herself and the symptoms that concealed these feelings from her. I particularly highlighted her early experiences of being left alone in the street, being left alone as the baby-sitter and feeling panic, and the steady self-derogation that finally became more than she could handle when her father died. From that point on, she turned her full energies toward doing for others in her attempt to please everyone and prove her worth. More than that, her behavior aimed at proving to herself that she deserved to live, but she could never get herself to believe it. I added that, since she felt her time was limited, naturally she chose a type of psychotherapy with a clear time limit.

> DOCTOR: For something to end, to say good-bye, means death to you . . . if I let you go, it means that you are bad, undeserving, and should die.
> MRS. T: I agree with everything that you've said except for the last part . . . my only concern is what will happen if it all recurs. . . . I've made a lot of progress . . . but will it hold?
> DOCTOR: You deserve to live.
> MRS. T: (Crying.) Every time you say that I just can't contain myself.
> DOCTOR: It is something that only you and I know.

I reminded her to maintain her self-esteem by being alert to her feelings of inferiority and to the contradictions between her achievements and her estimate of herself. Before she leaves, I tell her that she may find herself becoming angry with me at times and that she will know what it is about. She thanks me and spontaneously kisses me on the cheek.

First postscript

Little more than two months after termination, Mrs. T called to tell me that things were quite bad, that treatment had not helped her, and could she come to see me? She was promptly given an appointment.

She appeared smiling and obviously very much dressed for the occasion. Things had been very good for her until she and her husband had gone on an extended visit to members of his family who lived in another part of the country. She had not wished to go but had yielded. She had gone bike riding during the visit and had noted pain on the entire right side of her abdomen. The pain was intermittent and never sharp, and she became convinced that she had a malignancy. She had seen her gynecologist, who had found some pelvic tenderness. He had proposed more intensive investigation of her pain. She felt that it was all quite useless since it was too late. She would not consider X-rays of any kind because she would get cancer from all the radiation she has had over the years.

As she told me all this, I remarked that it seemed to add up to an intense feeling of helplessness—things had gone out of her control. She herself sees that her panicky feelings arise from her sense of helplessness. Once more I related the panic and helplessness to old experiences and feelings of being unloved and unwanted; she experienced these feelings with me when I let her go, but she conceals them with her body pain.

The interview pointed up the extent to which she defended against separation anxiety, with its catastrophic meanings, by developing somatic symptoms which, unhappily, carry the same catastrophic end. I gave her an appointment to see me again in a week, to give her time to digest what we had gone over today.

On her return, the separation issue was made the center of attention. She could say that she realized that she wanted someone to take care of her, to love her, to be with her always. She was angry that I had not warned her of what might happen after she left and then related a dream that revealed how she does things for people even when it is against her own interest and how she is abandoned nevertheless. The meaning of the dream was explored in terms of past events and as it related to me. I told her that my leaving her does not mean that I do not care about her and that she can work toward being separate and free. I added that, if symptoms appear, it will mean that she is concealing what are now familiar feelings. The meeting was characterized by active interchange. The dream in particular made the point for her, since it was, after all, her own creation.

Second postscript

Six and a half months later, Mrs. T called me. She was feeling very well and had no symptoms. The difficulty this time was in the marital relationship. Would it be possible for me to see both of them?

The couple was seen in four weekly interviews. It appeared that, with the removal of physical symptoms as her primary defense, she had now entered actively into a battle for parity with her husband. This attitude did not sit well with her husband, who was himself an active, controlling person. Thus, the battle for control was carried out by each inflicting pain on the other. Mrs. T was no longer able to somatize conflict and so the whole arena of their relationship had been altered. In the interviews, each came to appreciate how his or her honest wishes and needs were indirectly expressed by inflicting pain on the other. Nine months later, she informed me that the marital relationship was satisfactory, and she continued without physical symptoms.

Third postscript

Seven months later, after an interval of relative tranquility, marital difficulties again necessitated another series of four joint interviews. The husband was particularly insistent that treatment not be prolonged. The power struggle had reasserted itself. Both spouses wished to preserve the marriage, and a degree of resolution was reached. It was now apparent that Mrs. T no longer needed to resort to physical disabilities or to concern about fatal illnesses in her difficult relationship with her husband. The marital strife was producing depression, which previously had been concealed by her physical complaints and fears. She was aware of this change and acknowledged that she preferred the battle with depression to the previous defensive mode.

Fourth postscript

Three and a half years after completion of the original treatment plan, Mrs. T and her husband continue to have recurrent periods of friction, which derive primarily from the distress surrounding the problems of an adolescent son who has recently begun treatment with a child therapist. The boy is adept at inciting both parents into disagreements about how to handle and respond to his provocations. Mrs. T becomes depressed during these episodes, but continues to manage her home life and outside life very well. It is likely that respite will come when, with further treatment, the boy begins to come to terms with himself and with his parents. Family treatment may be indicated when the boy is ready for it.

It is evident from the foregoing that this has been a very difficult case. A long history of hypochondriacal preoccupations, reinforced by multiple medical examinations and self-imposed interruptions of psychiatric treatment on two earlier occasions, points up the complexity and difficulty involved. That she made gains in time-limited psychotherapy seems sufficiently clear; it is equally clear that greater gains would have been desirable. A considerable lessening of intense pain was achieved, but the patient continued to struggle and suffer over many issues. To summarize the dynamic changes, there was an expansion of effective ego functioning, along with an increase in self-esteem and a concurrent softening of her harsh superego. Would additional psychotherapy—time-limited or other—provide still further change? No such recommendation was made in view of my expectation that the boy's treatment would be followed or accompanied by family therapy (a plan that the boy's therapist also approved), which might offer her as much help as is possible.

7

Hysterical Character Neurosis: *Must I Always Be Second Best?)*

The patient discussed below illustrates some of the issues involved in time-limited treatment of a hysterical character. In this diagnostic category, powerful conflicts centering on rivalry with important past parental figures and siblings assume a central place in the determination of psychopathology. Repression serves as the major mechanism of defense. With the failure of various long-standing neurotic compromises, this patient's old, long-forgotten conflicts reemerged, causing the symptoms described below. Choosing the central issue in this diagnostic category, then, involves paying special attention to those aspects of the Oedipal conflicts that have been poorly resolved and therefore cause neurotic difficulty. In some patients these conflicts may involve directing attention to the difficulty in choosing their love object, closely related by displacement to earlier Oedipal wishes. In others these wishes involve primarily the aspect of rivalry, and in still other patients other issues, or even multiple issues, which bear most directly on aspects of the patient's conflicts that have not been resolved, and which are symptomatic of present behavioral difficulty. Because of this complexity, two cases involving the time-limited treatment of hysterical character neurosis will be presented.

In the second case of hysterical character neurosis to be presented, still another issue is involved: the relationship to the love object itself as a primary determinant in the etiology of certain character traits and in the development of a particular symptom. Here the overwhelming personality of an Oedipal love object caused far-reaching consequences in the development of psychopathology.

The central issues chosen in the two cases are quite different, yet both relate to the same level of development. What is discussed in each case is not so much instinctual conflict as such, but features of the hysterical character's object relations and their effects on self-esteem (through guilt and loss) and on character and symptom development.

After taking a careful and complete history, the therapist must discern what is of special importance to the patient so that the patient can relate to it experientially. Employing vague, broad generalizations that cover wide areas of Oedipal difficulty will not suffice in choosing a central issue. Conversely, choosing a narrow area of difficulty that does not include a significant portion of the patient's conflicts leaves unresolved problems.

L. A., a 33-year-old divorced woman, came to treatment complaining of "crankiness, impatience, and bossiness." A midrange executive in a company for which she has worked for the past ten years, this rather tall, attractive woman described a change in her personality about two years ago. Before that, she described herself as very patient and "easy to be with." She had always gotten along with people, rarely lost her temper, and never found herself in the irritable moods she currently experiences. Although she denied feeling depressed, she has become progressively "more unhappy with myself" for her irritability and impatience.

The patient is the younger of two sisters, born while her father was in the service; her mother was a housewife. When she was 5, her parents divorced; her mother and the two children moved back to the East Coast, where the family had originated. Father remained in the West. The patient remembered little of the divorce or of her parents before the divorce.

The patient described her mother, who is 63 years old and in excellent health, as an "Auntie Mame movie character. She's balmy, with a sense of the ridiculous, great fun, not too deep, doesn't know herself at all." Of mother's personality, she said, "I love it, except she's not motherly, she gives only platitudes, but she does give sympathy." She described her relationship with mother as close, but primarily characterized by having fun together. To illustrate, she recalled that, at the time of her own divorce, she and her mother went traveling in Haiti, where she "picked up a couple of pansies with me and had a gay time."

The patient's father is 63 years old; she said she knew little about him. She had seen him only about five times in the past twelve years. She visited him three times, and he came to the East Coast twice. About two years after her parents' divorce, her father married a "woman just the opposite of mother, she's motherly and very nice." Their marriage resulted in three children, two boys and a girl, whom the patient essentially never knew. She thought, however, that they were all doing well.

The patient described her father as a man who had wonderful stories to tell. Father told her he had been upset about the divorce but that "mother was hostile to men anyway." He said that mother thought men were "bastards and crumbs." She admired father who, after many years of working for a company, decided to go back to school at the age of 50. He achieved a Bachelor's degree, a Master's degree, and finally a Ph.D. He now teaches at a college.

The patient's sister, P, is 38 years old, unmarried, and in excellent health. The patient described her as very sharp and very bright. For as long as she can remember, she fought with P, who was very bossy and was always fighting with either the patient or their mother. The patient saw the sister as very selfish but very honest; the family treated the sister as if she were "very precious." Describing herself as inarticulate, she could never "fight it out" with her sister, who always won an argument. She was often jealous of her sister's successes, and on many occasions had felt like having it out with her, but was fearful of being unreasonable and of losing control. Although there were many fights with the sister, the anger was apparently one-sided; the patient "never got angry at her." She felt that in some indefinable way she and P were alike.

After many job changes, two years ago P began her own business, which quickly became a success. In addition, although P is unmarried, she does have a relationship with a married man whom she sees when she wants to. The patient regards P's business and romantic life as highly successful. There were obvious notes of jealousy, which the patient readily acknowledged.

When the patient was 11, mother married a man who is 73 years old. The patient was never close to her stepfather, who always felt that she and sister already had a father; thus he "never played the role." Yet she described him as a wonderful, sensitive man who was very fair, especially in his treatment of sister and her.

She related how stepfather drank heavily, but stopped when she was a teenager. He retired from his father's business when he was 58 and devoted himself to a specialized hobby. She described mother and stepfather's marriage as one in which they got along well but went their own ways. The patient defined this in terms of their having separate interests and in reality spending little time together. The patient remembered her childhood as a happy one. She had many friends and enjoyed school. She described mother as having had a number of boyfriends before she remarried, and one in particular who frequently abused mother physically.

Summers she would visit with her maternal grandmother, who has since died. She described her grandmother as "a very proper person who took a nap after lunch and who had very strict manners."

After her mother's remarriage, the family moved to a nearby city. Her sister was admitted to the same school mother had attended, but the patient could not get in. "I went to the second best school," she said, although she liked the school very much. Despite her feeling that she was as bright as her sister, her grade-point average was consistently just under sister's. And while P had gone to a four-year college, the patient had attended a junior college and then a secretarial school. After finishing school, she worked at one job for a few years and then moved to the company where she is now employed. She has achieved some advancement and pay raises, but she feels that her peers have done better. She said that somehow she lacked the aggressiveness necessary for further success.

The patient's menarche began at age 11. She "was glad it came" but remembered being told nothing about it by mother. She began dating at age 16, and shortly thereafter began seeing one young man whom she went with for two years. That relationship ended because of another girl; the patient remarked that she couldn't "fight the competition." She didn't date again until she was 23, when she met a man who was ten years older than herself. She liked him a great deal because he treated her "like I was a person." In some respects she had never thought of herself in those terms. She particularly liked him because he compared her to her sister, describing the patient as nice and her sister as a "bitch." However, he drank a lot and was unreliable. After about two and a half years, he moved to another city for another woman. Once again, she couldn't fight the competition. She described him as her first love; he was also the first man with whom she had sexual relations.

About a year later, she met and married a man six years younger than herself. She described him as a wonderful artist with no training; he was the artist she wished she could have been. She spoke of their relationship mostly in terms of her being motherly to him. Because he was "lower-class," mother and sister did not like him. Before long, the couple began to fight and grow apart; they were divorced two years after they were married. At first, she was rather vague about the fighting and the eventual divorce, but later, she acknowledged that he liked younger women and implied that he left her for someone else. Again, she had lost. In the four years since her divorce, she has dated a number of men, but until six months ago was close to only one. He was a divorced man with two children who, again, was "in love with someone else." It was with this man, however, that she finally had orgasm during intercourse for the first time.

Six months ago, she met a man two years older than herself. She became involved with him but, as with other men she had known in the past, she felt herself to be in competition either with other women in his life or with his interests. In any case, she felt she would lose. "My men are always in transition, growing, moving away." She emphasized that it was not merely that H's other interests were more valuable than she was, but that she did not have it in her to "fight and compete" with them. It was H who had heard of time-limited psychotherapy and suggested she seek it for herself.

The evaluation was completed in two interviews. It was clear from the patient's history that the diagnosis was hysterical character neurosis and that the central issue related to her inability to compete and to achieve success. Although many of the patient's difficulties may initially have been related to her relationship with her mother and her parents' divorce when she was 5, the central and ongoing issue since then has been her always having to come in "second" to her sister. Although it had always been a source of resentment, there was comfort in the idea that sister was not very successful and was a bossy bitch, while the patient was kinder, more patient, and more feminine. Two years ago, the equilibrium had finally been disturbed with sister's two major successes, the first in business and the second in her romantic life. The patient became angry, embittered, and more overtly jealous, a state of mind that was alien to her and left her feeling guilty and frustrated. As all these feelings came to a head in her relationship with H, where she again felt she could lose, she finally sought help.

The central issue presented to her was that she was tired of feeling second all the time, that she now wanted to be first but did not like the feelings that were associated with that, i.e., competitiveness, aggressiveness, and anger. Moreover, I told her the conflict seemed to have been a long-standing one that grew out of her relationship with her sister. She immediately agreed with what I had said, whereupon I suggested that we meet for twelve sessions to work on the problems raised in the central issue. She agreed, and a termination date was chosen.

Session 1

The patient began the first meeting by complaining that she had not seen H recently, that she had felt hurt by this and worried about their future. She added that she will be going to a resort to see an old boyfriend. Although she told this to H, the latter was not jealous, making her feel even more uncertain that he cared. She wondered what was happening between them and said she cannot get angry at him when he does not pay attention to her. She immediately remarked how her sister, P, does demand attention. At a party, her sister and H talked for a very long time, and she was left feeling excluded. She wanted to express her feelings but "I couldn't anyway, because jealousy is my problem." She added that "I guess I'd rather be a martyr anyway, the nice one." I asked about her playing the martyr. She said that in some ways she had always played that role in relation to both her mother and her sister, but especially the latter.

(I chose the martyr issue here because it provided an excellent opening into a discussion of some of the defenses she had used in dealing with her rivalrous feelings. Instead of competing, this patient had turned to self-denial and was in fact proud of it. Thus, by bringing up the martyr issue, I had hoped to explore her competitive wishes, the resultant guilt, and the neurotic compromise that followed, i.e., a masochistic solution. Her ambition was always just to be equal; she remembers always being afraid of being number one. She paused and reflected, "I guess I keep myself in the background.")

My comments centered on her fear of becoming "number one," her wanting to be equal and yet remaining in the background. I related all this directly to the central issue and pointed out how the martyred role had, in spite of its shortcomings, always seemed preferable to her, but that this was no longer the case. She now wanted to be more and to have more, but these wishes bothered and threatened her in a way not yet understood.

Session 2

The patient immediately began discussing her trip to the resort to visit her old boyfriend. As in the first hour, her thoughts focused on jealousy, but this time she wondered if her old boyfriend would be jealous of H, rather than the reverse. Indeed, she said her old boyfriend seemed hurt and she hated to hurt someone she liked. She and her old boyfriend had discussed P, and he had commented that "your sister was a problem for you." This reminded her of a recent meeting with some girlfriends, one of whom openly told the patient that she was jealous of the patient's "sexiness." The patient immediately told me, "That's O.K., I'm jealous of her for her brains and success." I pointed out that this was in fact one of the ways she had seen her sister and herself, with her sister having the brains and success while she was the sexy one. I also reminded her that this compromise was no longer working for her because sister had become successful in both areas. In addition, since she felt that H would require brains in a woman, she had to compete in that area as well.

She agreed with my comments and added that if she succeeded with both sexiness and brains she would have little to complain about in life. Moreover, she said she was fearful of sister's jealousy if she succeeded, but had become intolerant of failing again and was fed up with the "martyr role." Though part of her preferred the old equilibrium, part of her could not stand it.

Although the patient had previously agreed with the suggested central issue, for the most part she had only given her assent rather than articulating the problem herself. In this hour, for the first time she expressed the conflict in such a way that it was clear she was beginning to come to grips with it.

Session 3

The patient opened by saying, "I'm jealous of all women, I've discovered." She had made this discovery both by thinking about things and in a conversation with H, who had been teasing her about other women. However, she does not like feeling jealous: "It's too petty an emotion." She was reminded of a party she went to recently, at which one or two girlfriends were holding center stage. At such times she becomes quiet and somewhat withdrawn. This in turn reminded her of a particular girlfriend, A, who frequently holds center stage when they are together with a group of people. She never realized before how A reminds her of her sister P: "Both assert themselves and hold court."

She recalled stepfather's view of P as business-oriented and she herself as men-oriented, all reminding her of our last discussion. She said that people refer to her as P's sister; again "I'm in second place." With some irritation she remarked, "P can ask, demand, and I can't." She wondered where all that started and remembered a wealthy great aunt who seemed to favor P. Although she could relate few specifics about this great aunt, the impression of her favoritism for P remained. She further remarked that she had trouble demanding attention; because she feared she would lose her temper in making any demands, she kept quiet. This led her to discuss another source of her jealousy of P. P can somehow assert herself without losing her temper; moreover, this quality seems to result in P's success not only in business but with men.

Now the patient accepts the central issue more fully and begins to expand on it by relating events and feelings to it. The conflict is now quite clear in her mind, and she can ask where "all that started." At first she focuses on her aunt and establishes a connection between being favored and being able to ask for attention. She also begins to discriminate between assertiveness and anger and realizes they are not the same.

Session 4

She reported that she was down in the dumps today, and explained that she hasn't seen H for about a week. She was supposed to see him, but he decided to visit two friends, a married couple. H did not invite the patient because he does not like his friend's wife and did not want to subject the patient to her. The patient said this bothered her because she wanted to go anyway in order to be with H, but she could not ask him to include her. She remonstrated with herself for not being able to ask for anything. I pointed out that for her, asking seemed to be assertive, and she seems to associate assertiveness with anger, as we had discussed the hour before. She agreed with me and was reminded of how difficult it was for her to engage on equal terms in groups of women, especially if there were dominant women like her sister present. She added, "I can't fight with her, she'll say I'm too emotional." She went on to discuss with a great deal of affect how she could never ask for equal time in relation to P, and how P always won a fight anyway. She added that P was too smart and then reiterated her fear of losing control.

I reminded her again that she tends to confuse assertiveness with anger; the latter makes her fearful of losing control and of being totally ineffective. The theme of the third session continued, with special emphasis on competition with her sister, especially as it relates to self-assertion in any situation, but here specifically in connection with asking for time with a man she wishes to be with.

Session 5

The patient looked less depressed but did not comment on her mood. H had gone out of state the weekend before to visit an old girlfriend who was recovering from surgery. He had been apologetic but felt he had to go and complimented the patient on her patience. Although, realistically, she did not feel H was interested in his old girlfriend, she nevertheless was jealous and was aware that instead of fighting over that, "I picked a fight over something else, an inconsequential matter." She wished she could have controlled her anger better and expressed it over the real issue rather than a diversionary one. I asked her about this, i.e., her fighting over the diversionary issue. She replied that if she had fought over the real issue it would have exposed her "vulnerability," and if that were exposed she feared she would have become even angrier. I asked her if that reminded her of her sister and she replied emphatically, "Yes." To be so angry is to be a bitch, and to be a bitch is to be like sister. Her associations led from bitchiness to masculinity, and the equation in her mind of bitchiness and being a man—or, more precisely, a woman with a penis—was clear. Many people referred to her sister as "manly." So again, in her mind the alternatives were to be vulnerable and a woman, or bitchy like her sister, and a man.

For the first time the patient refers to her vulnerability, for which she sees no defense except withdrawing and remaining quiet. The only alternative is overwhelming anger and rage, which would identify her as a man, or as unfeminine, or as a bitch like her sister. Again, the confusion between assertiveness and anger is evident. Picking a diversionary issue is another defense against feeling vulnerable, which again could result in a loss of control.

Session 6

The themes discussed in the previous session were essentially repeated. She led off with her inability to assert herself with H; how as she became more involved with him she seemed to be able to ask for less and less. She said she was fearful of making demands and could not quite understand why, in view of our past discussion. She indicated that she was feeling more assertive in other areas, but that somehow the issue remained quite bothersome with H. After a period of some silence, she said that something had occurred to her. With a great deal of affect, she said that if she asserted herself with H, she would then leave herself wide open and vulnerable, and that this, as we had discussed before, she viewed with great anxiety. The emphasis here was no longer on the difficulty of asserting herself but on her feeling that if she asserted herself she would be left exposed and vulnerable. Her sister can assert herself with a man because "unlike myself, P doesn't have anything inferior about her to worry about." Here it seemed clear that the patient was referring to the old issue of brains and success in the business or academic world.

I pointed out the vicious circle the patient found herself in, and how it all related to the equilibrium she had set up very early in life with her sister. She confused being assertive with being angry and aggressive, which she saw as manly and therefore unfeminine. So in this respect she took second place, although she felt more feminine than P. However, this in turn left her feeling less capable than P in the business and academic worlds, and less capable even of asserting herself with men. Thus, if she wished to compete for a man like H, who admired success, in her mind it left her feeling inadequate and inferior, especially in comparison to a woman like her sister.

The further elaboration of the dynamics as they related to the central issue was attempted. If she were assertive about her wishes and expressed them openly, she would be left vulnerable and exposed. The latter was untenable to her because it would reveal what she considered to be her areas of inadequacy and inferiority, which in turn would result in H's rejection of her.

Session 7

The patient mentioned that she had been thinking about the woman who had surgery and whom H had gone to see a couple of weeks ago. In the past week, she had realized why she had felt inferior to this woman. The woman was a successful businesswoman like her sister. She related this insight with some satisfaction and then matter-of-factly announced for the first time that her father was in town visiting her this week. She had been upset when father told her that she was "first in his eyes." "I didn't like it, I don't want to be first, I only want to be equal." She noted that she immediately felt guilty and predicted she might feel worse if, unlike P, she could be both feminine and assertive. She had always felt that father saw P as intellectual and superior while recognizing the patient as feminine and outgoing. Yet she acknowledged that simply being first in father's eyes was pleasurable to her and that perhaps she did not have to deny her wish to be first any longer. I pointed out that perhaps she had been attributing to her father, to H, and to many other men her own values about what men want, which were in turn caused by her need to see herself as inferior and in second place.

In this session, she revealed how her guilt feelings about winning would not allow her to accept her father's putting her in first place. Finally, she could acknowledge both the wish to be in first place and the guilt that accompanied it. The task was to find new solutions to the conflict expressed in the central issue, rather than resorting to martyrdom or self-defeating behavior. In addition, she achieved further insight into her need to feel inferior. She would rather feel inferior, or second, than superior (to her sister), or first.

Session 8

The patient said that for the past few days she had been impatient, crabby, and angry. She did not quite understand why she was feeling this way. She had been feeling better after the last meeting, but, as the week

wore on, she gradually noticed her mood change. At first she related it to
H and her wish to live with him. His divorce is becoming final and he is
preoccupied with it. She said she had felt selfish in placing her demands
and interests over his, but realizing this feeling did not seem to change
her mood. She went on to discuss how her sister was enjoying father's
visit, but that father had reiterated his preference for the patient. Again,
she wondered if somehow this related to her mood, but she could not be
sure.

She returned to H and discussed her competitive feelings in respect to
H's daughter; the latter may deserve H's time more than she does. I
pointed out that it must be hard to compete with a little girl and that, in
the light of our previous discussion, she must feel selfish and demanding.
In fact, she had felt that way and seemed to acknowledge that the difficulty of competing with a little girl contributed to her mood. Yet she
wondered if something else were also present.

At this point I raised the issue of her feeling of impatience and asked if
that brought anything to mind. After some silent moments, I asked her
how many sessions we had left. She said, "Oh, four," and then added,
"you mean I want to hurry things up and get better fast?" I wondered
about that with her and she related how, in the past few days, she had felt
especially impatient and had had a vague feeling that time was flying.

In this session, she experienced a return of the mood for which she
entered psychotherapy. Although these complaints seemed related to our
present discussion, it did not seem to her enough to account for her
mood. Clearly, the fact that there were only four sessions left was uppermost in her mind, but it was kept out of awareness and warded off by an
exacerbation of her symptoms.

Session 9

The moodiness expressed in the last hour seemed absent. She spoke
mostly of father leaving and of H being away for his divorce. In spite of
both these events, however, she felt neither sad nor irritable. In the
course of the week, she did notice guilty feelings, because she had gotten
to see her father alone and sister did not. She had been feeling somewhat
successful in general and would like to tell her sister about her psychotherapy but had decided against it. She said, "I'd like to spring it on her."
She acknowledged now how she would like to change roles with her
sister. She concluded the hour by saying, "I'm finally tired of being the
little sister."

She did not mention termination, but clearly the interpretation of the
week before had had its effect. The irritability and moodiness had for the

most part declined because she realized she had made some changes. In effect, although she had felt that time was flying last week, this week she acted as if she had beaten the clock.

Session 10

She began by talking generally and vaguely about how, in a foursome, she flirts with the other man, although she says she is no threat to the other woman. When another woman flirts with her man, however, she withdraws and does not fight. She wonders again why she puts herself in second place and adds, "Maybe I really want it that way, to be a martyr like my mother." She added that perhaps she only likes the fight and the competition, that the challenge is more important than the man. Maybe the man is not so "full of riches," not so worthwhile in her eyes. I pointed out that, unlike the previous session in which she discussed feeling successful, now she was talking about putting herself in second place again and preferring to play the role of "a martyr, like mother." I also reminded her that her complaints seemed similar to those she had when she entered treatment. Moreover, she was introducing a new subject—that it is the man, rather than herself, who is not worthwhile. I asked her if she had any thoughts about my comments. She replied that she felt scared that there were only two sessions left, and that she realized she was introducing a new theme and recalling the old one as if it had not been discussed. She added, "I was thinking, maybe I liked this too much, maybe I don't want to quit."

Anxiety about termination now dominates. Unconsciously, the patient brings up old issues as well as introducing a new one in order to suggest that, with so much still to be worked out, she does not have to leave therapy after two more sessions. Here, it seems obvious that it is not simply therapy that she does not wish to leave, but more important, the therapist. Although she had been in therapy only a few months, strong transference feelings have been present. Now they seem more related to separation anxiety. It is likely that they also relate to finding in me her old heterosexual object choice, her abandoning father.

Session 11

The patient immediately mentioned that this was the next to the last meeting and said that she felt both good and bad about it. She felt good about it because she wanted to win now; she no longer saw being a loser and a martyr as solutions to her conflict. The least she would accept was a "fifty-fifty relationship." She discussed how for the first time she had been able to win a victory over H; she had overtly fought him over her rights to his time and had won. Moreover, she said, she did not feel the old selfishness or vulnerability that had claimed her in the past. She also remarked that her relationship to her sister seemed to have undergone some change. It was hard to define it, but she knew she was not as accommodating as she had been in the past. There had been some shift and her sister perceived it; her sister has begun to call her up instead of the other way around. She also said she had noticed the same positive changes in other areas of her life and was happy with what psychotherapy had done for her.

Yet, she said, "the bad part" was also bothering her. She was afraid of feeling alone and unsupported when she stopped therapy, and of slipping back into her second-place role, which she now rejects. I told her I thought she had made significant progress; now whenever she feels unsupported and wants to play the old role, she will have the knowledge and strength to see to it that she does not slip into her old compromise.

The patient reports significant progress in relation to her presenting symptoms and character attitudes as well as a deepening insight into their origins. She wonders, however, if the change can be permanent without the therapist's continuing support and encouragement. Here the therapist functions not only in his capacity of an old, libidinally invested object, but as an externalized superego she needs to have available to counteract her own inflexibility. My comments are aimed at supporting and encouraging her own ego capacity to deal with the archaic elements of her superego.

Final session

In the first part of her last session the patient spoke about recent events with H, relating how she had felt more successful with him but still could not be quite as forceful as she wanted to be. She feared being left alone by him. I reminded her that last week she had spoken of being left alone by me and remarked that this was indeed the last session and that she had made no direct mention of it. She said, "Yes, I thought of being alone in the past week, of not having anyone objective to talk to." She further related that she is scared, frightened about leaving treatment. At the same time, she related that she had another feeling, a feeling of confidence, a feeling that "I've learned a lot, in fact enough to help myself and also feel good. I really feel good, I've accomplished something." She added, "I know I'll have to keep working, but I feel much more confident that I can do it." I suggested to her that she had indeed worked very hard and had indeed accomplished a lot. I also told her that I thought she could do a lot for herself without me, that she was now quite objective about herself. She then thanked me for my help and shook my hand.

At termination, ambivalence about leaving the therapist emerges. Separation anxiety is evident and is responsible for the return of some doubts as well as the avoidance of talk about termination in the first part of the session. Nevertheless, it is easy to remind her of her gains and the causes of her anxiety. In fact, with just slight nudging, she reminds herself.

In my comments following the tenth session, I remarked on two strong determinants of her transference and the resultant anxiety on termination. This patient's history was characterized by a caring but shallow and unsupportive mother, and a father who essentially abandoned her early in life. In recent sessions, she made a number of references to feeling unsupported or alone and scared. These clearly related to her finally finding in me a mother who would care for and support her, and a father (and mother) who would not leave her alone. Thus, the separation anxiety alluded to in the past two hours is reconfirmed. Finally, she spoke of H and her fear of being left by him in spite of feeling more successful with him. Thus the displacement onto H of her concern about leaving me and being left by me. Here the therapist and H represent not an unsupporting mother but an abandoning father. In spite of her success with H, she cannot trust that he will remain with her because (aside from certain realistic considerations) her first heterosexual love object—her father—left her, just as I was now "leaving" her. Thus the strong possibility mentioned after the tenth session was further confirmed.

The unconscious does not recognize time. Very quickly, old and powerful wishes and feelings are placed on the therapist. On termination, they are frustrated, resulting in great disappointment. The hoped-for fulfillment does not occur in the transference. Real time confronts the ego. In essence, the ego must choose between an old solution, represented by symptoms, and a new solution, represented by realistic gratification and growth. It is in these last hours that the issue becomes critical and the task most trying for both the therapist and the patient. However he says it, the therapist must help the patient to recognize that she indeed has the capacity to grow.

Follow-up

This patient was seen for follow-up approximately two years after termination. She was quite enthusiastic about coming in for a follow-up interview. During the interview she was bright, alert, enthusiastic, and related quite warmly. There were no traces of the depression that had been obvious when she originally came for treatment.

When I asked her to comment on her work with me she immediately said, "I really feel much better." She described how she felt about and what she remembered of her work with me. She recalled that we attended mainly to her relationship with her sister and said that this relationship was much better. After therapy with me, she said, "I began telling her that this is how I feel, that these are my thoughts, you'll have to listen to me." She went on, "I wouldn't be second to her, I spoke right up." And then she finally added, "She is no longer a thorn in my side."

The patient described improvement in other areas of her life. She spoke of feeling much more relaxed in general as well as less nervous and much more assertive in her work.

She then described the only significant difficulty in her life since termination. A few months after termination she began to have increasing difficulty with her boyfriend. She could not decide whether to remain with him or leave him. He had become more inconsistent, less involved, and in general the relationship became more uncertain. "To sort out my thoughts," she entered psychotherapy with another therapist. Initially she went once a week and later once in two weeks. The therapy lasted about a year. The essential focus of the therapy was her boyfriend. She said she did not come to see me because, "Although I liked you, I wanted more time to work on the details of my relationship with him." The therapist was older, gave her direct advice, and encouraged and supported her. It was obvious that this therapist stood in the place of her father, to whom she was never close and from whom, therefore, she received no direct support or encouragement. As a result of her work with this therapist, she was able to break up with her boyfriend.

It was quite clear that her more recent psychotherapy served to complement the work already completed in the time-limited psychotherapy. As she described it, "I realized that when I left here I wasn't going to be in second place to my sister any more, and could assert myself as my sister did without being selfish. When I left here I knew enough; the other therapist helped me to put things into practice with a man; things had to sink in, I was slow." Time-limited psychotherapy, in addition to what it accomplished in regard to her sister (and derivatively her mother), had reawakened (through the transference) her wish for more time with a real father. And, indeed, she utilized the time of the second therapy to obtain paternal support and encouragement, which in turn increased her self-esteem and enabled her to terminate a relationship that was not in her best interest, i.e., with a man who was like her father—inconsistent, uncertain, and uninvolved. Before the time-limited therapy, the desire for a father and the loss of esteem accompanying the absence of important paternal support had been deeply repressed.

Regarding her sister, the gains remained and seemed to consolidate as time passed. In fact, if this significant relationship had not been resolved, in our opinion the possibility of a meaningful relationship with a man would have been foreclosed.

8

Hysterical Character Neurosis: *(Why Do All Men Brutalize Me?)*

The patient was a 29-year-old separated, part-time student, who was referred with the chief complaint of, "I'm separated and I am a virgin."

The patient described her difficulties as beginning about two and a half years earlier. At that time, she finally married a man with whom she had been going for about five years. Although he was confident and assertive in his professional life, she saw him as "kind and gentle, soft and passive" in his relationship with her.

Although she liked these personality characteristics and felt safe with him, the relationship lacked a romantic component and thus the relatively long courtship. One of her other concerns was that she had never had intercourse and was frightened of it. She and her fiancé had agreed not to have intercourse before marriage. This provided another reason for the prolonged courtship.

The marriage was difficult from the start. It continued to lack a romantic component and they were unable to consummate a sexual relationship. As she put it, "I would be terrified he would hurt me [on penetration] so I froze up. He, in turn, was afraid of hurting me." The patient was left feeling "frustrated and depressed." Nevertheless, the problems continued. She became involved in psychotherapy for about six months, with little result. She said, "I fell in love with the therapist and couldn't think of anything else."

About a year after her marriage, her mother, whom she had been extremely close to her whole life and whom she described as a kind, wonderful woman, died after a short illness. The patient went into a "state of shock" for about two months, followed by active mourning for a few months. A short time later, she began to fall in love with a professor in a school she was attending. This relationship remained intense on her part but platonic in reality. She described him as a wonderful, romantic man whom she just adored. As the crush on her professor grew, she became more unhappy with her husband and finally decided to seek a separation. Aside from not being able to have sexual relations, she had lost interest in her husband and compared him unfavorably to the professor. Five months before her initial evaluation with me, she separated from her husband. Nevertheless, her relationship with her professor did not improve and "I was as frightened with him as I was with my husband." With this she felt defeated and eventually sought psychotherapeutic help.

The patient is the youngest of five children, with three older brothers and one older sister. The patient described her mother as "a really nice person with a good sense of humor, who spent her life sacrificing for her children." She added that her mother and father had always fought bitterly, and that her father had "destroyed my mother's confidence; I always sided with her, I was close to her. It was very hard for me when she died." She recalled how her mother "always talked against men, she saw men as irresponsible babies who never helped out. My father, my mother told me, always treated my mother worse when my mother was pregnant." She added, "When my sister got pregnant out of wedlock when she was seventeen, my mother hated it, and talked about how horrible men were."

The patient's father, a recently retired stockbroker, is 64 and in good health. The patient described him as very cold, uneducated, but intelligent. She added, "For as long as I can remember he was ignorant and cruel. He would beat me up twice a week since I was a little girl for the smallest things. If I spilled milk, he would hit me. He hit me in the head, grabbed my ears. I always felt he was trying to break me." She added, "I'd never let him." She described her parents' marital relationship in the same terms: her father, who never drank or smoked, was rigid and unbending with mother, was always critical of her, and sometimes hit her, too.

The patient's two oldest brothers, twelve and nine years older than she, were both married and had children. The patient had little to do with them once they left the house but felt closer to them while she was growing up. She said, "They were like better fathers to me." The patient described being much closer to her youngest brother, who is five years older than she is. She said, "We were alike in temperament. I really liked him. Sometimes when I feel I need affection I want to put my arms around him." Although she does not see him often, the patient remains close to this brother, who is divorced and has two adopted children. She said she usually sees him when she needs help. She described her only sister, who is three years older than the patient and married with two children, as superficial and much like the father; the patient was never close to her. In reviewing her feelings about her siblings as a group, she said, "I'm glad my brothers were not like my father, they were much nicer."

The patient remembered little before the age of 5, other than living in the country and feeling lonely when her sister went off to school. The patient had little trouble going to kindergarten or the first grade, but she does remember feeling very shy. She was frightened of being called on by the teachers, especially if she did not have the right answer. In this light, she recalled her father "demanding I have the right answer. He'd yell and call you names if you didn't." It was from the age of 5, moreover, that she recalled her father beating her for the slightest mistakes. During this period, she began a pattern that continued until only recently, i.e., having one or two close friends and essentially not becoming part of a group. She now has developed many more friendships.

Her grades throughout elementary and junior high school were good, although she worried that if she did too well her youngest brother wouldn't be happy. She apparently had no direct evidence for this assumption. She did recall masturbating when she was a child, which alarmed mother. She remembered suddenly stopping, forgetting all about it until only recently. Menstruation occurred at age 13 or 14. She described feeling "relieved it came, I was worried, I thought it was late." Although she said mother told her about menstruation, she also felt mother was uncomfortable talking about sex. Shortly after menarche, she said she developed the idea that "sex was too confusing. I thought it was terrible. I decided I never wanted to have intercourse." She later added, "It gave me the impression that you had intercourse by a man punching a hole in your stomach."

During her high school years, father's beatings worsened so much that she began to do poorly in school and even failed a whole year in high school. She moved out of the house to live with her favorite brother and thereafter obtained excellent grades. In spite of her ideas regarding sexuality, she did date frequently, although she was never interested in having intercourse.

After graduating from high school, she worked for about a year as a salesgirl, but gradually found herself looking up to people with a college education. She managed to save enough money to attend a junior college, from which she graduated with high grades. After graduation, she worked in an accounting firm and attended college at night, which she has continued to do for many years. It was while attending college that she met the professor on whom she developed the crush described earlier. When she was about 23, she met her future husband, whose relationship with the patient has been described. Although she had many crushes on men from her late teenage years on, she was "terrified of sex" and uninterested in having sexual intercourse. She divided the men she liked into two types, i.e., those whom she was attracted to but afraid of, and those soft, kind, maternal men who did not attract her but who were "safe" and could be trusted. When she was finally married, it became clear that she did not trust the maternal type of man either. In this connection she said, "I feel sorry for my husband, he had to suffer for what my father did to me."

During the evaluation interviews, the patient appeared to be an attractive, bright, and warm young woman who had an enthusiastic manner and an almost childlike optimism. Beneath this, however, her sadness was obvious. She expressed both guilt and anger: the guilt was connected to her broken marital relationship, for which she took responsibility; and the anger was directed at her father for being the cause of her mistrust of men. In addition, she spoke longingly of her mother, whom she missed. Nevertheless, it seemed that she had done a great deal of mourning in regard to mother's loss. She stated that her treatment goal was to improve her relationships with men, especially in regard to her sexual problems.

The patient's history, character, and symptoms all pointed to a diagnosis of hysterical character neurosis. Intensely identified with mother, she saw men as brutal and enslaving; she was terrified of them and unconsciously enraged at them. This conception of men clearly resulted from her own relationship with her father, from witnessing father's brutalization of mother, and finally, from mother's view of men. As she said, "I feared being dependent on a man, I didn't trust them. I felt pity for my mother my whole life. The only reason she stayed with father was because of five kids. She never had a life of her own because of the five kids." In view of the patient's brutal history, we must assume that her relationship with her brothers, especially the youngest, provided the only psychological basis for her developing any libidinal interest in a man.

With the above in mind, I suggested time-limited psychotherapy with this central issue: "That no matter how much she has tried, she has been unable to modify or change her feeling of mistrust of men; that this arose out of her victimization by her father and that this feeling has left her feeling hopeless and inadequate." The inadequacy, I explained, was related to the fact that, though she felt she should trust some men—for example, men like her brothers—she was unable to do so. She readily accepted the central issue and immediately spoke of her fear that with men "I won't be able to be in control of things, I couldn't be in control of my life; women get pregnant, and men aren't dependable. But I do want to have relationships with men, I'm worried I won't be able to."

Session 1

The patient entered the office appearing somewhat shyer and more nervous than during the evaluation interviews. She was again dressed plainly, a characteristic which lasted through most of the psychotherapeutic process. She described how a lot of her friends were emphasizing looks and how some of them were leaving the area. She spoke of feeling unable and unwilling to attempt to look attractive and said she preferred friends who emphasized other characteristics. In this light, she said, "I need new sources of support, I'm glad to be here." With that she began to discuss her worries about her inadequacy as a woman compared to "men's weaknesses as men." She said she oscillated between feeling herself to be inadequate and feeling that men were inadequate, and she could not tell which bothered her the most. She spoke of her fear of "a man getting control" of her life, and of her concern that she would lose control and become too dependent on a man. My comments during this first interview mostly took the form of encouraging her to continue with her thoughts. In the course of the interview her initial nervousness and shyness disappeared, and she became much more at ease.

In this interview the patient was both stating the central issue and elaborating on the themes involved. Moreover, she was alluding to her beginning relationship with me. In that vein, she wondered whether I would be a support or simply another man whom she mistrusted and had to battle.

Session 2

The anxiety and shyness noted at the beginning of the first interview were absent. She continued on the theme of her fear of becoming dependent on a man. "I'm afraid I'll lose control of myself and get involved with a man again." She immediately began talking about her relationship with her father and again spoke of the frequent beatings he inflicted on her. She spoke of her mother's slavery and oppression by father. "I hate the idea of getting married, I don't need a man." I pointed out that, although she may feel she doesn't need a man, another side of her feels that she would like to have one. After this comment, her mood changed; she became somewhat more subdued and said, "No, but I am afraid I just can't please one man." She then continued to discuss the themes involved in the central issue, i.e., her fear that her mistrust would get the better of her in any relationship with a man, thus leading to a repetition of her relationship with her husband.

In this interview the patient's mood and content both demonstrated her significant denial of the central issue. This was evident during the first part of the session in terms of her elation and denial of any desire for a man. As a temporary phenomenon, this kind of denial is not uncommon during the initial phase of time-limited psychotherapy, and in most patients it is easily clarified so that the patient can again focus on the relevant dynamic issues. The denial also represented a wish to avoid dependence on the therapist, who chose, as in the first interview, not to interpret it at that time. The therapist felt that the patient simply could not hear an interpretation; it would only tend to cause more resistance to the developing transference.

Session 3

The patient continued to discuss her feelings about marriage. She no longer denied her wish to have relationships with men and possibly get married, but she again mentioned her mistrust and hatred of her father, which carried over to all men. She again reviewed the many discussions she had with her mother regarding father's enslavement of mother following their marriage. During this discussion she referred to her father as "Mr. B." Her anger mounted as she described in detail the multiple beatings she had sustained from Mr. B. She was obviously disowning him as he had earlier disowned and betrayed her.

She suddenly thought of sex and said, "Sex is a trap, it's bad enough to get involved with a man, but once you have sex with him, it's a prison." I reinforced what she was already coming to realize; that a woman could be enslaved to a man by the temptation of sexual pleasure as well as by children. Thus, if she avoided sexuality, she could avoid imprisonment. The patient readily accepted my comments.

This meeting brought out and later reinforced an idea that the patient had not been fully aware of, i.e., that a person can imprison herself not only because of external circumstances such as children but also because of her wish for gratification. Moreover, the clear implication was that, in seeking gratification, a person cannot protect herself from dangerous situations such as the one her mother experienced with her father. I emphasized the patient's mistrust both of men and of her own sexual desires, which she feared would lead her to the kind of imprisonment her mother suffered.

Session 4

The patient opened by saying how depressed and sad she felt because "the professor" had just gone on a trip for a few weeks. Although they did not even date and saw each other only sporadically in and around her school, she described feeling rejected and angry. Although she knew these feelings were out of proportion with their actual relationship, she nevertheless could not contain her sense of rejection and anger. She spoke of hating men for controlling her life. She described having suicidal thoughts on hearing of the trip but explained, "I wouldn't do anything like that." I discussed with her how she had blamed the professor for going on a trip, and therefore controlling her life, even though there was no close relationship between them. I wondered whether she might be upset about the intensity of her feelings and concerned that she could not control her involvement no matter what the real nature of the relationship was. I pointed out that she must feel out of control in these circumstances, and consequently feel humiliated and inadequate. We further discussed how she unconsciously blames herself, then projects that blame on the man, and finally cites her father as the cause of it all. The patient was involved in the discussion and seemed to assimilate what was being said. She left feeling much better.

In this session, the patient continued the theme of mistrusting her own libidinal wishes and her fear that, once she allowed them expression, she would not be able to control her level of involvement. It was critical that her repeated projections onto men—blaming them for her own lack of control—be dealt with in this hour. Without discussing this feature of her defensive structure, her repetitious complaints about father would have continued, preventing forward movement. No matter how much he had contributed to her present mistrust, she could not improve until she saw herself as less helpless. Her use of projection did not permit that to happen.

Session 5

The patient began this meeting by discussing a young man in whom she felt interested. Although she liked him, she said she did not experience the "crush" she often feels on beginning any relationship. Although she was clearly being careful not to let her feelings get out of control, her reaction was now more appropriate than it had been in comparable situations in the past. She neither withdrew immediately nor became prematurely overinvolved. Indeed, she seemed almost proud of herself as she described the control she was exerting over her feelings. She expressed "having to keep the upper hand over Dave [the new man she had met]; I won't let him get control of me." She again discussed her feelings about father and exclaimed, "I have to do it, because of him." I said that I did not disagree with her about the reasons for her keeping the upper hand, but I added that she was appropriately also keeping the upper hand over her own tendency to become involved too rapidly.

In this session, although some projection is still manifest, the patient is clearly struggling to control the premature intensity of her involvement in relationships. In doing so, she is controlling both her childlike naiveté and the power her libidinal wishes have over her. In this way, she experiences less helplessness and as a result sees men as less tyrannical and enslaving. She is slowly realizing that some of the entrapment she had felt in her relationships with men was indeed her own doing.

Session 6

The patient started by wondering if I disliked her. I asked if she could say more about that. She said she had no idea where it came from, she had been happy with the psychotherapy so far, but that thought just seemed to be in her mind. She went on to say that in all of her relationships with men, she always thinks of being rejected. She added, "That's why I won't have sex with them, that would be total humiliation, to be rejected after having sex would be terrible, at least this way I save something of myself." Although she had never discussed or acknowledged any positive feelings toward her father, her associations immediately led to him again; she recalled the constant sense of rejection by him, which made her feel worthless and abandoned. She described feeling that father had always "disliked" her.

For the first time in the psychotherapy I made a direct transference interpretation, linking the feelings she expressed toward me at the beginning of the session to the feeling of dislike she felt father had toward her. Moreover, I wondered if she did not experience this fear of dislike with men in general. After some thought, she said that it was always present. I also suggested that, although she did not mention it today, she was developing a new relationship with a potential boyfriend, Dave. I suggested that this could also be playing a role in her worry about being disliked.

As noted, in this session I made my first direct transference interpretation, which she accepted readily, thus confirming that the timing was correct. A premature interpretation of transference material can lead to increased resistance. With this particular patient, who was so frightened of the power of men, premature interpretations would only have led to a feeling of being attacked and/or to the eroticization of the transference. On the other hand, to have waited any longer would have served no useful purpose; in fact, material that could have led to important and helpful interpretations would have been bypassed. Ignoring this kind of material at the wrong time in time-limited psychotherapy can permanently forestall its emergence.

Session 7

The patient opened this session by announcing that her brother's girlfriend had become pregnant and had had an abortion. The patient was extremely upset and felt that her brother's girlfriend had been victimized by having to go through such a trying experience. As the patient discussed the incident, she became furious and attacked her favorite brother as being like all men. It brought back memories of her sister's pregnancy at age 17, which had provoked mother's fury and her condemnation of men. Further discussion made it clear that neither her brother nor his girlfriend blamed the other, that they both regarded it as an unfortunate mistake and were continuing to see each other. Although both of them were unhappy about the abortion, they had both wanted it and had not complained. At this point I confronted the patient with that fact and wondered about her blame; that is, if neither her brother nor his girlfriend blamed the other, what made it such a powerful blow for the patient? I also wondered, if her brother was indeed such a nice guy, what was the realistic basis for lumping him with all men? These were rhetorical questions aimed at helping her think about her need to project onto men and her wish to undo the previous gains in psychotherapy. Although there was some upset, she seemed to accept my comments and listened attentively as the session came to a close.

In this session, the patient attempted to rescue her old defenses and undo some of the work accomplished in the previous hours of psychotherapy. Certainly the incident with her brother reverberated deeply in the patient's unconscious, with its associations to mother's pregnancies, which both mother and the patient saw as enslaving mother to father, and to sister's unfortunate pregnancy. It occurred to me that another unconscious factor might have determined this reaction; namely, the fact that it was the seventh session and termination might have been on the patient's mind. Since the material did not lend itself to this interpretation, I waited for a more appropriate moment.

Session 8

The patient began the meeting by talking about submission. She went on to discuss some of the familiar issues she had talked about previously: mother's submission to father, her fear of submitting to her own impulses and also to men, and the incident mentioned in the last session regarding her brother's girlfriend. As the session proceeded I noted that although she seemed involved in what she was talking about, there seemed to be a somewhat sterile, repetitive quality to it. I wondered again if she were not displacing some of her feelings to these areas from the psychotherapy itself—more specifically, from the transference and from termination, which was fast approaching. With this idea in mind, I pointed out that it was the eighth session and she had thus far made no comments about termination.

She suddenly became silent and for a few minutes said nothing. Finally, after I asked her if she would tell me what was on her mind, she said, "anger." She felt she was in a struggle with me and that "I wanted to talk about another thing." I suggested that perhaps what she wanted to talk about and what I wanted to talk about were related. Her anger abated somewhat and she began to think about what I had said. She said she noticed "a fear in me of your being angry at me." She noticed that when she felt that fear she developed a stomachache. She reflected on how similar stomachaches occurred whenever she thought her father or former husband made any demands on her.

She wondered why she was reacting to me in this way. As she thought about it, she realized that "you weren't making the demands, you were just asking me a question. Why did I react that way?" She added, "I know it's crazy intellectually." At this point I merely reinforced the relationship between me, her father, and her former husband in her own mind, and suggested that such strong feelings toward me also must bear some relation to this being the eighth session, with only four sessions remaining. I also suggested that her stomachaches might represent both a strong wish to please me and a very angry reaction against that wish. To want to please me would put her in a position of vulnerability which—as with her father, her former husband, and her new boyfriend—she most steadfastly wanted to avoid.

In this session, she was experiencing with me the struggle she had experienced with her father, her former husband, and other men, including her current male friend. The session was most useful in that she could notice the similarity of reactions and could also experience affectively the connection between her feelings toward me and toward others from the past and present. A minor issue regarding what to talk about in this session became a major war for her. Her awareness that her feelings were irrational was a major step toward beginning to separate past from present, father from others, and therefore old imprisonments from new potentials.

Session 9

The patient began by saying she "wanted to express feelings at others' expense, not my own." She remarked that this led to her wish to blame others, because if she did not blame others she would have to blame herself, and she did not want to be a victim anymore. In spite of her noting her "crazy" reaction to me last week, which she saw as inappropriate to the situation, she still noticed how very much she wanted to blame me and see my question of the eighth session as a "tyrannical demand." She realized that she just wanted to be angry at me. I pointed out that her reaction of not wishing to be a victim was certainly understandable in the light of her past. I also pointed out that she might be feeling like a victim again, insofar as termination was just three sessions away. Her remaining comments were less about termination and more about her usual angry reaction to men. Without further explanation, she spoke of how "self-destructive that attitude is, look at my reaction to my brother over the pregnancy, it could have ruined a good relationship." She was now confronting herself in the same way that I had confronted her in the seventh session. As she left the office she exclaimed, "This was a very good session."

Although I felt that the patient had already made significant progress in psychotherapy, this ninth session seemed to be a major therapeutic turning point, in which there was an obvious assimilation of earlier insights and interpretations. In addition, her confrontation with her own self-destructiveness indicated a positive identification with the therapist—a necessity in any successful psychotherapy.

Session 10

The patient entered the office looking particularly bright and cheerful. She said she had an announcement to make about which she was very pleased. She then exclaimed, "I did it" and smiled broadly. It soon became clear what she meant. One evening during the previous week she had had intercourse for the first time in her life. She discussed how she and Dave had been talking about the possibility for the past couple of weeks and finally decided to try it. It worked. "More than that," she said, "I enjoyed it." There was none of the terrible anxiety and overwhelming paralysis that was evident in the previous attempts at intercourse with her husband. She was not frozen as she had always been and felt that her attitude had changed considerably. She described feeling very proud of herself, and her mood and tone reflected that pride. Most of the session was taken up in her discussion of the "triumph." When I asked her what she felt had allowed her to succeed, she readily gave credit to the work accomplished in psychotherapy, which has lessened her mistrust of men and increased her comfort with her own libidinal wishes. Although she felt she had significantly improved, she implied that she also had more to talk about—a clear reference to the topic of termination, which we had not yet discussed.

The "turning point" noted in the comments after the ninth hour was dramatically confirmed by the events in the succeeding week. Her ability to have sexual relations for the first time was a reflection of the change in her attitude toward men and toward her own libidinal wishes. As was discussed earlier in reference to the central issue, her neurosis had had a devastating effect on her self-esteem. Because of her mistrust of men and her unconscious hatred of her own wishes toward men, she had felt entirely inadequate as a woman. Her elation at being able to have sexual intercourse clearly indicated one of the sources of her damaged self-esteem and how it was improving. To have treated her solely as a victim might have helped her somewhat, but it would not have rid her of her feelings of helplessness and inadequacy. In turn, her self-esteem would have remained low.

It must be pointed out that her having sexual relations at this time also had the meaning of acting out. That is, because of her anger at the therapist for rejecting her through termination, she chose to obtain from someone else what she couldn't have from the therapist. Given the principle of multidetermination, this "acting out" should not be viewed in any way as detracting from the therapeutic gain noted above. But unless her angry feelings related to termination were worked out, her symptoms might return. A revival of symptoms did not seem likely, especially in view of her work in the following sessions.

Her sexual behavior illustrates our earlier observation that acting out, if there is any, is likely to occur in the tenth or eleventh session and be clearly related to the transference distress caused by the impending separation and loss. The therapist must be alert to this kind of response from the patient and ready himself to handle it directly.

Session 11

During the previous week the patient had gone on a trip to see friends in another state. She opened this session by relating how, on her return from her vacation, she began worrying that "Dave might reject me." There was no hint from Dave of any such attitude. She related that, although she remained quite happy over the success she reported last week, she was preoccupied with her worries about Dave. I reminded her that this was the eleventh session, that only one remained, and that perhaps her feelings about Dave had something to do with her seeing termination as a rejection by me. She reported that she noticed immediate resentment at my comment, but she was able to observe her resentment and gain insight into it. She said that she treated me as she did other men; she did not want to become vulnerable or dependent. She fought against vulnerability in her relationship with me but also had noticed that she liked me and would miss coming to therapy. It was clear that for her this was a significant admission, one she could not have made earlier without overwhelming humiliation or embarrassment.

This session was characterized by an initial displacement to Dave of her feeling of rejection by me because of impending termination. Although she still resisted positive feelings toward the therapist, early in the hour she could admit to vulnerable and affectionate feelings for Dave. It was an important sign of her improvement that, although she noticed resentment when I suggested that she might feel rejected by me, she nevertheless was able to acknowledge her affection for me. Further, she acknowledged her affection without feeling overwhelming embarrassment or humiliation, which in the past would have stimulated the use of denial and projection.

Session 12

The session began with a rather prolonged silence. When I asked her if she could comment on her silence, she replied that she had been wondering about me. She said that she was thinking about what I was like, what I did in my everyday life, whether I was married and had children. As she spoke I noticed how her total appearance had changed over the course of psychotherapy. Previously she had dressed rather plainly, as if to hide her attractive features. In this hour she was dressed very attractively without appearing seductive. She went on to say that she had felt affection for me and would miss coming to psychotherapy. Nevertheless, she did not feel any sense of rejection or belittlement by me, nor did she notice a romantic crush on me. She felt "quite happy with my psychotherapy here" and said that she had "accomplished an awful lot here."

I took this opportunity to discuss with her what she had in fact accomplished, and reminded her of the pitfalls of regression to her old ways of feeling about herself and relating to men. I reviewed with her the origins of her deep mistrust of men, the inhibition of her own sexual and affectionate feelings, and how she had previously relied on denying that she had positive feelings for men to ward off intense feelings of vulnerability, humiliation, and shame, which belong to the past relationship with her father. I also reminded her of how she had so consistently blamed others that she rendered herself more helpless and inadequate. She listened attentively, expressed optimism about her future, and thanked me for the help I had given her.

The patient's attitude reflected significant overall improvement during her psychotherapy. Along with her own positive reaction to the psychotherapy and her expressed optimism about her future, the evidence for significant change was clear. On entering psychotherapy, her appearance was that of a shy, anxious teenager; she now looked like a mature woman. In addition, she had been able to have sexual relations for the first time. Her attitude had gone from intense mistrust of men to a positive acceptance of them, without her feeling overwhelmingly vulnerable and frozen. Although it was clear that her old feelings were not entirely absent, it was also obvious that they were less intense and that she had significant control over them.

I believe her improvement during psychotherapy was related primarily to the interpretation of her intense use of denial and projection, the resulting emergence of previously repressed affectionate and erotic feelings, and the development and interpretation of the transference insofar as she unconsciously experienced me as her father. As she came to like and trust the therapist, she was able to separate past from present, father from therapist, which in turn enabled her to develop the beginnings of a new attitude toward men and toward herself.

Follow-up

The patient was seen in follow-up more than four years after termination. On my greeting her, she smiled broadly and seemed quite happy to see me. She related that "since I last saw you, I've wanted to call you a number of times to let you know how well I was doing; I'm glad you called." She had been doing very well in both her work life and her relationships with men. She said that for the past four years (until one month ago) she had worked for the same accounting firm and done extremely well. Some time ago she decided that she would like to open her own firm and had done so one month ago. She felt elated at the opportunity for independence and success.

In regard to her relationships with men, she said that she had remained with Dave for about three years after termination. Although she cared about him and had a good relationship with him, she decided to break up with him because he could not commit himself to a more lasting relationship. Some time after that, she went with another man for a short time but soon saw that "that relationship wasn't for me." At the present time, she is beginning to date another man to whom she is extremely attracted; she thinks she would like a more permanent relationship with him. But mostly, she says, "My attitude toward men is much different now. I'm much more confident. I don't have those crushes anymore; I see them as fantasy. I see men much more realistically now—not the greatest or the worst. I like myself much better, and because I like myself, I can see other people as equals." She would like her future to include both career and marriage.

She then described how she had felt since termination. "I've been growing and changing. Before therapy, my self-esteem was such that I saw myself as a failure; I don't do that now. A failure is just a small failure, I personally don't feel a failure anymore. I have a completely different perspective now, I want to look out more for myself." She went on to describe how, in general, the old feelings of inadequacy have almost disappeared. She added, "If problems do come up, I can handle them and grow because of it."

I asked the patient in what way she related her improvement to psychotherapy. She replied, "I feel it was very successful. I can handle problems now as they come up. More and more the problems I had when I came to see you, like my father, receded into the past. I used to see him as all to blame, but I can now see other causes. And I now feel he couldn't help it. All of that came out of treatment. Therapy really made me feel it was in the past; everything we discussed in my present life at that time was connected with my father and me. I can separate other men, other people, from my father. I'm not confused now, I'm not confusing other men with my father. It's liberating." She went on, "And talking to you helped me talk to others. I like to get deep with people; in that way I missed you. Many times I wanted to tell you how well things have gone."

In addition to the changes in object relations and self-esteem, the patient reported no recurrence of the sexual difficulty she had experienced before psychotherapy. She had continued to have satisfying sexual relations with Dave and also had successful sexual relations with the man she was briefly involved with after Dave.

I also asked her how she felt about the time-limited aspect of the psychotherapy. She replied, "I thought about that. I felt you really did a good job. If you had let me lean on you, or if the therapy went longer, I think I would have gotten more dependent on you," and in effect not have achieved the sense of confidence and independence she was seeking. She continued, "After termination I would see other people going into treatment who had been in treatment before. I wondered why. I felt I didn't need it. I really felt I could handle my own problems." At this point, the session was just about over. She left expressing confidence and hope for the future, just as she had expressed her optimism when she terminated time-limited psychotherapy.

The significant changes that occurred during the psychotherapy had remained and widened in the intervening years. Separating father from other men, past and present, and not seeing herself as the helpless victim were crucial in this patient's improvement. It is noteworthy that these significant and dynamic changes did not stop at the termination of psychotherapy but continued long after psychotherapy was over.

Also of note were the patient's comments about the time limit itself. To have prolonged the therapy would have induced a more regressive, dependent transference, which probably would have been long-lasting, with significant detriment both to her self-esteem and to her relationships with others. Seen in this light, time-limited psychotherapy allowed for considerable maturation without the hindrance of a prolonged, disabling transference, the resolution of which in once-a-week long-term psychotherapy would, at best, be unnecessarily arduous.

9

Hysterical Conversion
with Depression: *(Why Do*
They Hurt Me?)

The case of Mrs. R has been selected not only to illustrate the treatment
of a conversion symptom but also to demonstrate how the selection of the
central issue as a statement of the patient's present and chronically endured pain gives entree to the patient's inner life regardless of differences
in color, religion, and socioeconomic status between therapist and patient. Close adherence to the central issue throughout the treatment establishes a thoroughly compatible mode of communication, even with a
patient who is not particularly given to verbal expression.

The positive transference, which develops quickly, allows the therapist
to inquire about the patient's very different background in a constructive
way, so that the patient experiences the inquiry as part and parcel of the
helping process rather than as a potentially shameful or demeaning exposure. In turn, the therapist comes to understand those aspects of the
patient's background that are alien to the therapist's experience. It is the
therapist's obligation to learn the language of the patient. In this mode of
brief psychotherapy, one can learn the patient's language without class
lines being an obstacle to "talking treatment."

Mrs. R is a 54-year-old black woman who had come to Boston from
Georgia four years earlier. She had been referred to the Psychiatric Clinic
by the primary care unit because of her depression and numerous somatic

complaints. The latter included headaches, backaches, swollen and sore ankles, and a chronic cough. She had been suffering from these complaints "for years." She is the mother of seven children and is separated from her husband, who remains in Georgia. She came to Boston with her youngest son after he graduated from high school. Within a week of her arrival in Boston, she was hospitalized for ten days, presumably because of "bursitis" in one ankle. Since that time she has been followed at the arthritis clinic, although a definitive diagnosis has not been made. Two years ago she began steady visits to the primary care clinic, where she was tested for possible hypothyroidism, hypertension, and a mildly symptomatic hiatus hernia. She has been taking Valium to help her sleep.

In the intake evaluation, Dr. W found Mrs. R to be alert, oriented, and cooperative. Her memory was good, her fund of knowledge adequate, and there was no evidence of a thought disorder. She was overtly depressed, as evidenced by her slow, very quiet speech. She did not express any suicidal ideation, and her appetite and sleep were reasonably good. Dr. W concluded that a major issue for the patient had been a terrifying episode some ten years ago. One of her brothers had come to her house in a drunken state and demanded the use of her car so that he could go to town to kill someone with whom he had been fighting. She had refused to give him the keys, whereupon he had opened fire on her and her house. She was successful in preventing injury to herself and her children. During the fray, she asked her husband to steal out and get the sheriff. He did steal out of the house, only to disappear and not return with help. For obscure reasons, the patient's sister, who had been a witness to the incident, said that it had been all the patient's fault, and from that point on the patient's mother and other family members blamed her. Her relationship with her husband deteriorated so much that she eventually left him and moved to Boston, where several of her children were already living. A diagnosis of depression was made and she was referred to our seminar on time-limited psychotherapy where, with her consent, she would be treated on closed-circuit television; each session would be videotaped for further study.

The first session began with a brief discussion about the television camera and who it was that was observing us. She assured me that the setup was entirely agreeable to her.

DOCTOR: Tell me . . . what is it that you most want help with?
MRS. R: I don't know . . . I can't remember things well . . .
There is some things I'd like to forget and some things I'd like to remember.
(*Having learned from the evaluation interview that her memory was good and, more important, that she had endured a very painful episode, I chose to pursue the "things" she wished to forget.*)

She then told me that her brother tried to kill her and that, when it was all over, the rest of the family sided against her. It was all very fresh in her mind and she simply could not understand the turn of events that made her the victim. The recollection troubled her and she became tearful as she discussed it.

> (*It is important to note that, although she had been referred to psychiatry because of depression and somatic complaints, she promptly turns to what had been a most painful and frightening episode in her life. She had never mentioned this to anyone in her years of clinic treatment. Experience has shown that some patients feel that they are not supposed to speak of their emotional problems in any of the medical or other specialty clinics. All too often it is the psychiatrist who provides the first such opportunity for the patient.*)

DOCTOR: Is forgetting this the most important thing to you?

MRS. R: Yes, it is . . . but the most important thing is that my mother died with that.

She then says that when her mother died six years ago, she still held the patient responsible.

MRS. R: She still died . . . when she died she was still . . . she didn't have too much to do with me.

DOCTOR: When she died she didn't have much to do with you for the same reason?

MRS. R: I guess it was the same reason. (*She begins to cry quietly.*)

DOCTOR: And that hurt too? And you would like to help forget some of this and you would like help with the hurt that you feel ever since your mother died . . . when she died she still held this against you?

MRS. R: That's right.

> (*Two significant points have been touched on: the shooting episode and the fact that her mother not only had sided against her initially but had died still blaming the patient.*)

Asked about other complaints, she told of her chronic cough, which often keeps her awake at night and for which medicine has not been of much help. Adding further to this unusual story, she said she would like to return to Georgia for a visit but that something happens to her there that makes her sick and forces her to return to Boston. She feels that something down there is bad for her.

> (*Another puzzle is touched on here. Something happens to her in Georgia that she cannot explain and that clearly agitates her. We get a first inkling of a somatic response to whatever upsets her in Georgia. In this first interview, it is enough to identify the various problem areas and to assess which of them merit intensive exploration in coming interviews.*)

We review her life in Georgia during the fifty years she lived there. During her last six years there, she had driven a school bus. Earlier she had worked on her father's farm and then on her husband's farm. In describing how hard the work was, she begins to cry. It was so hard and she had gotten so little schooling—only up to the sixth grade. She feels very bad about that and says that if she had had some learning she could have done more for herself. She blames her parents for keeping her at work on the farm.

DOCTOR: Do you feel dumb? Do you feel like you're dumb because you didn't get much schooling?

MRS. R: I feel if a person don't have any education then I guess that's what you have to call it. (She cries again.)

DOCTOR: When did you begin to feel sad about not having more schooling?

MRS. R: I regret it when my kids ask me questions and I couldn't answer them.
(*The fact that she was black and from a rural area of Georgia suggested that I should learn more details of her background, which was quite different from that of our typical clinic patients. She reveals a hard life and minimal schooling. That she should bring up her lack of education points to its importance to her. The therapist's statement that she must feel that she is dumb, expressed gently, is empathic because it says that the therapist knows how she has always felt about herself.*)

We review further details about her current circumstances. A number of her children live in and around Boston and she appears to have good relationships with them. She lives alone, however, and is not very happy about that.

DOCTOR: You're very lonely and you're always feeling very hurt, aren't you?

MRS. R: I don't know whatever cause it to feel that way.

DOCTOR: As I understand it, you have had a very difficult struggle and here you are . . . you're fifty-four years old and feeling very lonely and very hurt.

MRS. R: I guess that's it.

DOCTOR: Would you like to work on that problem to see if you can't find some way to handle it so that you'll feel better about yourself?

MRS. R: I sure would.

I then outline a treatment proposal of twelve sessions ending on January 9. She accepts the plan.

The interview ends with further details of her hard life in Georgia, her distress about her lack of education, and her determination to stick it out in Georgia until her youngest child finished high school. More information is also obtained about her family relationships. The central issue was formulated tentatively on the basis of the data obtained by Dr. W in his evaluation interview and the corroborating information brought out in the first interview. The central issue was stated and the treatment proposal outlined to her. The statement of her chronic pain made sense to her and she promptly accepted the treatment plan. Her background is such that one might believe that she would not be likely to challenge the treatment proposal, particularly with a white physician. Later events in the course of treatment substantiate that the statement of the central issue—rather than compliance based on her color and background—was the key to her acceptance. This point is emphasized to show that this method of formulating the central issue transcends the color, religion, and ethnic background of both therapist and patient.

She starts the second meeting by saying that she has been feeling a little better this week but that her cough continues to be very troublesome.

MRS. R: Doctors can't seem to find the trouble what's causing it.

DOCTOR: Do you worry about it?

MRS. R: I do, it worries me . . . at night sometimes I don't rest . . . I cough so much more than in the day.

DOCTOR: Do you bring up anything when you cough?

MRS. R: No . . . it just seem like there is a tickling . . . a sore space right there.

DOCTOR: How long have you had this?

MRS. R: Lord, I don't know . . . for years now . . . about ten or twelve years . . . if I could get rid of this cough I think I might make it a little better . . . it's so nagging.

(Her cough is of very long duration and we are not likely to learn any-thing more about its possible emotional sources at this point. We can explore its origins later in treatment, after the central issue has begun to open up the emotional conflicts that have led to somatic symptoms as attempted solutions. I therefore return to the present and direct her atten-tion to the ongoing process. I ask her whether she has thought any more about what we talked about last week.)

She says that she has been thinking about her brother, her mother, and herself. After she and her brother had had their "falling out," her mother had not only taken sides against her but had never forgiven her or regret-ted siding against her. About two years after mother died of a stroke, the patient left for Boston. Mrs. R had taken her mother to the hospital when she was stricken and had hoped mother would say something to her.

DOCTOR: Were you expecting that she would say something and forgive you, or forget, or come over to your side at least?

MRS. R: Well, I feel like she should have said something about it . . . some-thing . . . I wasn't in the wrong when all this happened and I just feel like if I turn against somebody for something they didn't do no wrong and I should die, I would feel like I wouldn't go to heaven. (Cries)

DOCTOR: And so you don't feel that she went to heaven?

MRS. R: I really can't see how she could have . . . I feel that she didn't make it to heaven that she did like she did.

(We learn that one of her religious beliefs is that entry to heaven is barred to one who dies without forgiving those on whom the deceased has inflicted

hurt. It would follow, of course, that if mother is barred from heaven then she must be elsewhere—hell, for example. At this point, however, no attempt is made to pose the obvious; since the patient has said nothing about it, the therapist suspects that she is defending herself against this blatantly obvious conclusion.)

After mother's death, Mrs. R decided that she would leave for Boston just as soon as her youngest son graduated from high school. The session continues with the therapist carefully exploring details of the patient's family: where her children are living, the patient's living arrangements, and the chronological sequence of the patient's migration to Boston. Chronology is important in order to ascertain the relationship, if any, between external events and the patient's emotional responses to those events. She then introduces an intriguing problem; she would like to visit or live in Georgia but something prevents her from doing so.

DOCTOR: What made you decide to stay in Boston?

MRS. R: I don't know . . . I can't understand that. I went back home twice since I've been up here . . . I think of staying there and then I'd be right back up here . . . I do this all the while and don't know what's going on . . . I wanted to go back but like I couldn't go back.

DOCTOR: If you had your own way, where would you be?

MRS. R: I think I'd be in Georgia.

DOCTOR: You have any imaginations about what might have happened?

MRS. R: I tell you . . . I did have an old lady that I know . . . she used to be my midwife with my first kids and she told me that someone had did this to me . . . but I don't believe in that.

DOCTOR: The midwife said someone did this to you . . . kind of put this feeling in you that made you leave?

MRS. R: They had me run off the bus and run for home . . . but I don't know how anybody can do that . . . run me off the school bus I was driving and made me run for home too . . . (Cries.)

DOCTOR: Against your will?

MRS. R: That's right . . . that's the way she said it was . . . evil . . . I don't know how anybody could do anything evil like that.
          (Something mysterious has driven the patient out of Georgia. One might expect superstition to be part of the rural and religious background of this woman. She suggests that some kind of hex might have been placed on her that forced her to flee Georgia. All of this is respectfully accepted by the therapist and used to clarify the nature of the patient's chronic pain.)

The interview continues with the patient relating that, before she left for Boston, her husband had told her that people were saying that she was planning to sell the house, take everything in it, and move to Boston. She could not understand what was going on, so she abruptly packed and fled to Boston right after her son's graduation. She misses the house in which she had invested so much effort. She has since learned that her husband claims full ownership and plans to deprive her of all property rights. She feels helpless about the legal possibilities and hopes that her children will go to court and get it straightened out. She feels that her husband has hurt and cheated her out of the home that she worked so hard to buy with him.

(A number of loose ends are brought together. She is not living in Boston entirely out of her own desire: there are real reasons that prevent ~~her~~ from going back to Georgia. In addition to whatever superstitions she may have, she also has a problem with her husband and the home she fears she will lose. Her story takes on the substance of a tragedy. She works long and hard in the fields and then on the school bus. She marries and has a family. Her brother, mother's favorite, attacks her. The patient spurns him, and mother never forgives her for doing so—not even on her death bed—despite the patient's pleas. Mother dies and the patient is driven from her home. Now she cannot go home and feels lonely, hurt, depressed, and hopeless.)

She appears for the third session with a soft orthopedic collar around her neck. She had been told to try it to help soothe her persistent cough.

(The cough is of obvious concern to her, and I attempt to make some inroads into the meaning of this chronic symptom. I do not expect to gain too much in this regard at this time. I give her an opportunity to tell me about the cough in terms of all the physical discomforts it provokes in her. My aim is to loosen her associations so that exploration of the meaning of the symptom might become possible.)

DOCTOR: Do you ever imagine to yourself what could be causing it?

MRS. R: I don't know.

DOCTOR: Do you think of it as something bad?

MRS. R: Sometime I do . . . sometime I don't know . . . I just feel like it must be something bad . . . but I'm not sure.

DOCTOR: Something bad like what?

MRS. R: I don't know . . . some kind of disease or something I have in my throat . . . like cancer or something like that.

(I could establish only that the cough has the meaning of something bad in her and concluded that we could go no further with it at this time. I then turned to the shooting incident to elicit more details, because there did appear to be some relationship between the shooting and the onset of her cough.)

She describes in detail all the characters involved in the shooting as well as the events themselves. Although it happened a long time ago, the patient's intensely affective response tells us that this is the long-festering hurt that, superimposed on other hurts, has brought her to her present state. The central issue has now been delineated much more specifically.

(It might be well to note here that the therapist should not only follow the patient's associations but also allow himself to associate to the productions. There is room, too, for the therapist to exercise his curiosity. I am referring not to the kind of curiosity that has as its aim the gratification gained from hearing intimacies of the patient's life, but rather to a curiosity about the details of situations and events that will

enlarge the therapist's understanding and that, incidentally, often contain important information that the patient has withheld, suppressed, or repressed.)

Fourth session:

DOCTOR: How are you today?
MRS. R: I'm feeling pretty good today.
DOCTOR: What do you have to say today?
MRS. R: I don't know what to say today.
DOCTOR: Have you given any further thought to what we were talking about last time?

(Because time is limited, an important technique in holding the patient's attention to the central issue is to inquire about the patient's reaction during the week to the preceding session. This is particularly helpful when the preceding session has been strongly affective but the patient shows no great inclination to talk about it.)

The patient's response was to the effect that she had thought of nothing that we hadn't talked about already. Further efforts to obtain additional information from her about the shooting incident were fruitless.

(I then began to pursue a series of questions that had puzzled me after I studied the data of the preceding session. I wondered why she had not told her mother and the others her version of what had happened. Had she done an "un-Christian" thing in refusing her brother the use of their car and equipment? Was that the first time she was considered the bad one in the family? Did anything happen during the fight that she has not told anyone, something she might be ashamed of? In long-term psychotherapy, we might patiently await answers to such questions. In time-limited psychotherapy, each of these questions is related to the central issue, and their answers will actively be sought.)

DOCTOR: You never told you mother your side of the story?
MRS. R: No, she didn't ever come and say anything . . . and I didn't think it was my place to go to her.
DOCTOR: Really?
MRS. R: I didn't thought it was . . . I didn't do anything.
DOCTOR: But you knew that she blamed you.
MRS. R: The way I see it, she knew what happened . . . she know how he went on and acted at her place to get the gun . . . and they tussled with him to keep him from carrying the gun out of the house . . . they know he come to my house, and when they come and get him, I was standing in the middle of the floor, blood running all over my shoulders, feet cut up and everything . . . they didn't ask me anything . . . didn't ask any of the children hurt . . .

Further discussion makes it apparent that Mrs. R's stubborn pride in view of the felt injustice was enough to keep her from protesting. Her mother lived on one side of her and her sister on the other side; both ignored the patient after the shooting. I suggested that she must have felt snubbed. She agreed and added, without saying so explicitly, that in spite of the bad treatment by her mother, it was she who took her mother to the hospital. She tries to be good and to win approval despite her hurt. I then further sharpened the central issue by remarking that she must have felt that she didn't exist as far as mother and sister were concerned.

We then turned to the relationship between her and the brother who had shot at her. He was six years younger than the patient; she had loved him dearly when he was growing up. She said that she could never refuse him anything until he began to use the farm equipment that she and her husband had bought and, through his misuse, threatened to destroy it. At that juncture, she felt that she had better intervene. The decision to say "no" to him came when he was drunk and was followed by the unhappy events described.

(Every effort must be made in these early sessions to gain as much information as possible about the important persons in the patient's past and present life. This woman is not the kind of person who would tend to pour out her recollections, nor was she likely to respond with a flow of associations in response to a question asked of her. I would not expect her background to have stimulated a highly verbal style of communication. I have no hesitation, therefore, in engaging in an active question-answer dialogue with her. The questions, however, are not random; they are always directed by the consideration of who were all the people who had hurt her and what they were like as she experienced them.)

My next line of inquiry referred to her own nuclear family, what it was like growing up as a child. She told of a family in which violent behavior was not unusual. She felt scapegoated by several of her siblings and described how she had used her fists when they ganged up on her when the parents were out of the house. When the parents returned, her siblings would unite in their accusations and the patient would be harshly whipped by her father. There were many such whippings. Whether or not this portrayal was factually accurate, the patient revealed her sense of being unjustly victimized long before the shooting incident. The patient related that once, in a fight with her brother (not the one who shot at her), she cut him superficially with a knife. After telling me this, she spontaneously added that it was wrong of her to hate that way. All of these details support the assumption that she is not just troubled by guilt about her own behavior; she is even more troubled by her anger and hatred.

DOCTOR: You were whipped more than any of the other kids.

MRS. R: I know I did . . . but hate was the wrong thing.

DOCTOR: Did you take the whippings and say thank you? That wouldn't be natural, would it? Did you ever know or did you ever feel that you did hate them for all the whippings?

MRS. R: I didn't feel like that I did.

DOCTOR: Have you ever hated?

MRS. R: I don't feel like I hated . . .

DOCTOR: Well, you must have hated your brother when you cut him up.
MRS. R: No, I don't feel like I hate him . . . I was just taking care of myself.
DOCTOR: You've never hated?
MRS. R: I hope I didn't.
DOCTOR: It's not a crime, you know.
MRS. R: I don't like hate . . . I feel like it's a sin to hate (cries) . . . I don't feel like you should hate people.
DOCTOR: Have you sinned?
MRS. R: Not that I know of.
DOCTOR: You have no sins at all?
MRS. R: I don't know . . . maybe I have some . . . but I don't want to have sins.
DOCTOR: I'm not talking about wanting to have sins . . . do you feel that you have any sins at all?
MRS. R: I've never done anything quite as bad as to have any deep sins . . . maybe . . .
DOCTOR: Have you ever had any nasty thoughts about something or somebody?
MRS. R: I don't . . . the only thing I feel like . . . if you don't like me just leave me alone . . . don't care for me . . .
DOCTOR: How about when you don't like someone?
MRS. R: I don't dislike nobody . . . I feel like it's people that I really don't trust . . . but I just don't just dislike them . . .
(Now we see the role of denial as a major defense against the anger that was naturally provoked by so many of the events she described. I press her and at the same time pose my questions about hate so as to indicate that hate might be quite a natural human reaction. She resists and reveals that she has at least two ways of managing her anger: she projects and finds that there are people who simply should not be trusted; and she withdraws—"Leave me alone, just don't care for me.")

At this juncture, I introduced a question about trust because I had noticed that she simply never looked directly at me. My question brought her to tears again, although she could not say what it was that kept her from looking at me. I continued to press her; something must be bothering her since she not only could not look at me but continued to cry. I reviewed all the injustices she has endured and how she has always been the goat in the family in order to reinforce the therapeutic alliance and soften her denial. Slowly I pressed her to look at me, even though we had not learned just what it was that kept her from doing so. With great effort she finally did so. I asked her if she was frightened when she looked at me, and she said that she was not.

(I had noted all along that she never looked at me and, in the light of the trend of this interview, I felt that it would be important to learn whether this was an indication of her lack of trust in me. Could it be that she was unable to trust my caring about her? Or was the discomfort that of a black woman with a white doctor? Or, as is often the case, did she fear that her eyes would reveal her badness? I also felt that it was in the

best interest of the therapeutic alliance to approach the question of eye contact directly.)

Having gone as far as seemed possible in the matter of eye contact, I then relieved her distress by moving to a subject she can handle easily although I know that it, too, is related to the central issue.

DOCTOR: How have you been feeling this week . . . how is the cough?

MRS. R: It's been doing pretty good . . . seems like it's a little better this week.

DOCTOR: Has it kept you up at night?

MRS. R: Just one night there . . . I think I'm better.

DOCTOR: All right . . . shall we go on further next week?

MRS. R: Yes.

(We are able to close the interview with the patient in better control of herself.)

She comes for the fifth meeting saying that if she had been able to contact me she would not have come today because she is not feeling well. This time she tells of a new complaint: upper abdominal pain that the doctor says is due to gall bladder disease; she must have an operation. A date for surgery has been set for some weeks hence. Her complaint suggests that we are seeing a reaction to the feelings aroused in our last interview. Somatization, already seen in her chronic cough and some of the symptoms she describes as occurring on her visits to Georgia, alerts us to her present complaints as another effort to defend via her body, even though the doctor said that she has gall bladder disease. The immediate relationship of the new symptom to the preceding week's session warrants such an inference.

Since she is unable to offer any substantive information of her own, I decide that the difficult week may be related to an intense reaction to my asking her to look at me, even though she had also spoken of all the turmoil that had occurred years before and that still haunted her so much. I chose the eye-contact problem because it was an immediate relationship problem rather than one that she had to recall from the past.

Slowly and patiently, I seek to learn the meaning of her not allowing herself to look at me. At this point, I am considering two possibilities. The first, and less likely, is that a paranoid delusion lurks in the background. The second, the one that appears to be more consonant with her past experience, is that there is some connection between this symptom and hints that she has made about strange interventions by people back home. Such strange interventions are not paranoid; rather, they are shared superstitions and so are culturally supported and acceptable.

DOCTOR: I'm wondering if we can get at this and see whether it's the same kind of feeling you have that keeps you from going to Georgia

where you would like to be. You'd like to look at me but you can't
. . . you'd like to go to Georgia but you can't.

MRS. R: It sure is . . . it seems the same.

DOCTOR: Are you saying that just to say it or do you believe it?

MRS. R: No . . . I believe it 'cause like I know I can't go to Georgia and I
don't know why I can't look at you . . . I don't see why I can't look
at you . . .

DOCTOR: Do you feel it's something that you don't have control over?

MRS. R: That's right.

DOCTOR: So it comes from somewhere else?

MRS. R: As far as I can see that's what it is . . . it comes from somewhere
else . . . I can't . . .

DOCTOR: Where do those things come from . . . if it comes from somewhere
else, where does it come from? You know about those things.

MRS. R: I heard people say a lot of things like that but I don't believe such
things . . . I've had people who tell me that people had me run off
the school bus and not come home . . . that's all I know.

DOCTOR: Tell me what else you've heard.

MRS. R: I've heard tell of people being sick and they didn't know what was
wrong . . . and go places and the people sickened something like
. . . I just don't like that . . .

DOCTOR: How does it take place?

MRS. R: I really don't know how it takes place but I know that it do take
place.

DOCTOR: What does someone do to sicken someone else?

MRS. R: I know one time my sister's husband was going out with another
woman and he put something in her yard near her mailbox . . . and
the mailman came along and her daughter went out to get the mail
and she fell . . . she couldn't stand for you to touch her . . . if you
walk across the floor she would scream and holler . . . they just
scared her some way . . . she got all right and my sister said that it
was good it was her daughter . . . if she would have stepped over
she would have fell dead right there . . .

She then speaks of people running others off their jobs because jobs were
so scarce.

MRS. R: . . . the kids used to come on my bus with oranges and apples and
they'd give it to me . . . but I never would, never did, eat these
things . . . she was an old lady . . . about eighty-nine years old and
she said to me, I'm glad you didn't eat those things those kids brung
on the bus for you . . . I said, why? . . . She said, you throwing
death out across the woods . . .

DOCTOR: You threw death?

MRS. R: After I put off all the kids and I'm going home I throwed them out
through the window across the road and she said that if I would have
eaten them it would have killed me.

DOCTOR: I guess you knew that you shouldn't eat them.

MRS. R: Something must have tell me not to eat them . . . I don't know what it was but I know I didn't eat them . . . it would have killed me.

DOCTOR: I think I can understand now that you've been frightened a very long time . . . I guess you're always frightened.

MRS. R: I guess so. (She begins to cry.)

(*Through a somewhat circuitous route that began with her fear of eye contact, we have been able to explore strongly held convictions that she is evidently very wary of exposing. The combination of my curiosity and my hunches, fortified by the presence of a positive transference, finally allowed her to reveal shared beliefs that were terribly frightening to her. Symptoms and an adaptive behavioral style effectively obscured from others as well as from the patient her profound dread of sickness and death inflicted by others possessed of ill will. She has long been a frightened woman, and it is likely that her fear has been the chief reason for her inability to look at me.*)

We then return to what is the greatest burden of pain for her. It was painful enough that her brother had shot at her and that all the family had sided against her. Most painful, however, was her mother's failure to forgive her before she died. She felt blameless, but she had been unable to gain any consolation from that. I am led to wonder why, in the face of felt blamelessness, her mother's failure to forgive continues to be such a persistent source of pain. Posing the two sides of the issue—blamelessness and no forgiveness—I ask myself what the patient must be feeling as a consequence. It would be entirely understandable for her to be angry, but again, her symptoms, coping style, and background would militate against conscious awareness of anger; in its stead, we should not be surprised to learn that guilt and self-blame are importantly involved. And so, with the feeling that enough groundwork has been done, we come around to the crucial question that the patient had raised much earlier in the treatment.

She describes answering the phone one day and being told that her mother had died. She felt numb and cried.

DOCTOR: As you think of it now, do you know why you cried?

MRS. R: I just felt like she died and she had never said anything to me about the way I did . . . (begins to cry) . . . I felt like she should have said something . . .

DOCTOR: But she didn't . . .

MRS. R: No . . .

DOCTOR: And as a result she has not gone to heaven?

MRS. R: I hope she did . . . I don't know . . .

DOCTOR: And you feel that she has never gone to heaven as a result?

MRS. R: Well, that's the way I feel about it.

DOCTOR: Then where is she now?

MRS. R: I don't know.

DOCTOR: Where does someone go if they don't go to heaven . . . is she in hell?

MRS. R: I guess it's not but two places to go . . .

DOCTOR: Then she's in hell?

MRS. R: I guess so . . . I don't know . . . [I hope so] . . . I hope not . . .
(The patient said "I hope so" so quickly, and corrected it so quickly, that I did not hear the angry wish. Only when I replayed the videotape did what she had said become clear. Thus I did not pursue this most painful subject, feeling that we had done a good deal of work on it. Not wishing to drift off to something so unimportant as to interrupt the intensity of the patient's emotional experience, I chose a second or third order of intensity, and we concluded the session with the suggestion that she continue to try to look at me.)

In the week preceding this sixth meeting, the psychiatric resident who had seen Mrs. R when she first appeared in the psychiatry clinic learned that Mrs. R had been scheduled for elective gall bladder surgery in the coming week. I suggested to the resident that he speak with the surgeons about our wish to complete Mrs. R's treatment first. They agreed to postpone surgery.

Mrs. R said that she felt somewhat livelier since our last meeting and that it was agreeable to her that the surgeons had postponed her surgery.

Still seeking to uncover further reasons for her inability to look at me, I made it a point to discuss further questions that I had in mind. For example, there was the possible importance of the difference in our color and the feelings long engendered by such differences. Her response and the tone in which she stated it left no doubt that this was not the case. Shame, another feeling that could be operative, was also explored with her. I accepted her denial of ever having felt shame and searched instead for another feeling that could evoke shame—anger. The discovery of the slip of the tongue about her mother in the previous session made this a logical path to follow. We had learned, too, of her long-standing fears about the strange things that seemed to be happening to her in Georgia. Wherever there is fear there is also anger, and given a background of both violence and fear, one can be certain that anger has an important role.

DOCTOR: You mean you can't think of anything that might have happened that you would be ashamed of . . . like even very angry thoughts about somebody?

MRS. R: I can't think of anything now . . . right now.

DOCTOR: Maybe you can't think of an example now, but do you think that it could have happened to you that you would have had some angry thoughts about someone?

MRS. R: No . . .

DOCTOR: You must be kidding me.

MRS. R: I don't know . . . probably I've been angry about something or other . . . things that people do to me . . . but I could never stay angry with anyone . . . maybe I did and didn't know it.

DOCTOR: You have some very good reasons to have been very angry.

MRS. R: I don't like being angry.

DOCTOR: I know that . . . you told me that to be angry is a sin . . . hate is a sin.

MRS. R: That's right . . . that's the way I feel.

DOCTOR: So you must feel that you're a sinner?

MRS. R: I don't feel like a sinner . . . I hope I'm not.

DOCTOR: Well, if to be angry is a sin, then maybe one of the things that's been bothering you all this time is that you do have some feeling that you're a sinner . . .

MRS. R: Anyway, I don't feel I'm a sinner . . . I don't feel like anything I ever did was really bad.

DOCTOR: If you were angry, is that bad?

MRS. R: I guess it is . . . it is bad to be angry with anybody.

DOCTOR: Are you a saint?

MRS. R: No, I don't think so.

DOCTOR: I don't think so either. I think you're more like the rest of us . . . are you sinful?

MRS. R: I couldn't say as I were or not . . . I don't like sin.

DOCTOR: But maybe you have reason to be angry?

MRS. R: I know I had plenty reason to be angry . . . so I guess I'm sinful.

DOCTOR: Can you accept yourself as being sinful?

MRS. R: I don't know.

DOCTOR: I can accept you as sinful because you had very good reason for being angry . . and you're only human.

MRS. R: That's right.

DOCTOR: And you were very much hurt.

MRS. R: Yes, I have been . . .

(The reader may feel that the patient is being compliant in order to avoid further pressure. However, more than enough data have been obtained from the patient to warrant vigorous encouragement. The data told me which direction to take. Knowing the direction, I had to make an estimate of the state of the transference and of the patient's ego strength at this point. If she had been truly paranoid, or even if she had displayed a circumscribed paranoia, it is unlikely that the direct approach would have succeeded. Note, too, the support given the patient in terms of her right to be human like the rest of us and therefore her right to have untoward negative feelings that she fears are forbidden.)

She then says that being angry with someone for something that person does to you is not as bad a sin as the sin of the person who does it. She is now ready to talk further about angry feelings: she speaks of her anger toward the sister who lived next to her in Georgia and who now lives in the patient's building in Boston; and then of the murderous brother, now living in New York. She doesn't trust any of them: "A burnt child is scared of fire."

DOCTOR: There is somebody else who hurt you even more than your brother.

MRS. R: Hmm . . . I guess there's my mother . . . nothing I can do because she's dead now.

DOCTOR: Maybe you were just as angry at her . . . even angrier at her than your brother.

MRS. R: I hope not . . . she is dead.

DOCTOR: But she did something bad to you.

MRS. R: That's true . . . she really did . . . I couldn't do like she did . . . to act up like that . . . when my brother did me . . . kind of hate to tell if one was wrong but I'd have to tell if he was wrong.

DOCTOR: But she never did, did she?

MRS. R: She never did.

DOCTOR: Well, maybe she's where she deserves to be now.
(The appropriate point has been reached to bring to the patient the major source of all her feelings that have been channeled into somatic symptoms and depression. We come to this point in the sixth session for the following reasons: (1) the time limit demands a degree of activity greater than may be one's usual style; (2) the formulation of the central issue in terms of the chronic pain has rapidly brought the patient into a positive transference and working alliance so that, although she is someone who has learned to trust no one, she nevertheless trusts the therapist; (3) the data obtained have led us to it; (4) we will need the remaining sessions to work through this relationship to the mother as well as the issue of termination.)

DOCTOR: Do you realize, Mrs. R, that you're saying to me that you understand now that your mother hurt you a good deal . . . something you would never do to one of yours . . . and that you've been angry with her all these years?

MRS. R: I guess so.

DOCTOR: And you'd just as soon she were in hell for what she did to you.

MRS. R: I guess so (deep sigh).

DOCTOR: How could you punish her for what she did to you?

MRS. R: The only thing I could do is to pray . . . to make the Lord take her off my mind.

DOCTOR: Maybe you can also help to get her off your mind too and help the Lord a little bit . . . where is she?

MRS. R: I guess she's in hell, I guess.

DOCTOR: Who put her there?

MRS. R: I guess she put her own self there, 'cause I didn't do anything . . .

DOCTOR: You were angry with her.

MRS. R: I know . . . I don't see that I should have gone to her 'cause I didn't do anything.

DOCTOR: I agree with you.
(The work has been to help the patient identify her feelings. She is given justification—the right to have particular feelings. We can then go on to examine her feelings of guilt about her wish for her mother. We know that people who somatize have difficulty in being aware of their feelings. The process of somatization includes the addition of symbolic meaning to the somatic symptom or symptoms.)

DOCTOR: How about when you cough up and nothing comes up. What's in there? Did you ever think there's something in there that you wanted to get out?

MRS. R: I do that . . . that's true . . . I cough and nothing come up . . . sometimes I cough till I gag.

DOCTOR: And is there the feeling that you're trying to get something out?

MRS. R: That's right . . . sometime I feel like when I swallow . . . I feel like I'm swallowing a ball or something in there . . . something feel like a lump or something in there.

DOCTOR: Like something stuck there?

MRS. R: Mmm . . . that's the way it feel.

(This appears to be a rather classic instance of globus hystericus. Perhaps she herself will integrate the feeling of anger, which she is now aware of, with my question about something bad inside her, and further, with the lump in her throat that she seems unable to eject.)

MRS. R: Sometime I just wish they would . . . I feel just get away from all of them.

DOCTOR: Go back to Georgia?

MRS. R: I'd rather be down there.

DOCTOR: You certainly got a bad deal all along, haven't you?

MRS. R: Well, I told them I wouldn't let that worry me 'cause dirt is dirt.

DOCTOR: What do you mean?

MRS. R: They don't even bury you in six feet of dirt any more . . . they put you in these vaults . . . you can't stay in the ground.

DOCTOR: You've been angry all these years for the bad things that were done to you and it's been bothering you and making you feel bad about yourself.

MRS. R: I guess I have (sighs).

(She looks directly at me as she leaves.)

The seventh session opened as follows:

DOCTOR: How are you doing?

MRS. R: I have a sore throat since yesterday afternoon . . . feeling pretty good except for this sore throat.

DOCTOR: How's the cough?

MRS. R: That's about the same.

DOCTOR: Do you remember much about our meeting last week?

MRS. R: Yes, I do.

DOCTOR: Maybe you'd like to tell me what you've been thinking about it.

MRS. R: I don't know . . .

DOCTOR: What was it that you most remember about our talking last week?

(It is worthy of note that, having made some small headway into the symbolic meaning of the cough, she now comes in with a sore throat, which follows excessive coughing. I chose not to ask directly about the cough since I could expect denial. Instead, I ask her what it was that she most remembered about our previous meeting in the effort to tap what might well be uppermost in her mind at this time. Posing the question in this open-ended way will diminish the patient's ready defensiveness.)

MRS. R: Worst thing . . . I really didn't know I had . . . I was angry at nobody . . . and that's really one thing I really thought about . . .

that I've been all these years like that . . . one thing is I was glad I knew it.

DOCTOR: You were glad to know what's been hurting you all these years.

MRS. R: Right . . . I didn't thought I was . . . I know it's a bad thing to be angry with people . . . I guess when anybody do things to you, you will get angry, but I didn't . . . I just feel like it's wrong to be angry.

DOCTOR: Well, it's not a very good feeling, is it?

(I paraphrase her statement that it is wrong to be angry by saying that being angry is not a very good feeling. I say this to help her focus on what she is feeling rather than letting her continue to use the issue of right and wrong defensively.)

We then talk about her mother, and I question whether she was angry with her mother even before the shooting incident. She used to think her mother was wonderful, and as we continue it becomes apparent that here, too, she is exercising much denial. In fact, she tells of numerous beatings for which she felt scapegoated by her siblings. Mother seemed never to believe the patient when fights broke out among the children, and the patient was invariably blamed and beaten.

(The active exploration of the patient's past points up the contradiction between the total sense of victimization and the absence of felt anger or the right to be angry.)

DOCTOR: You were mistreated . . . she never believed you . . . she blamed you even when your brother did what he did . . . and you never knew that you were angry with her?

MRS. R: No, I didn't.

DOCTOR: But when you were with her . . . how did you behave . . . how did you act with her?

MRS. R: I don't know . . . I just always did have a funny feeling when I was around her.

DOCTOR: A funny feeling?

MRS. R: Just that I felt scared some . . .

DOCTOR: Do you remember anything nice, pleasant of your mother doing with you or to you?

MRS. R: No . . .

DOCTOR: Really? She was always mean?

MRS. R: I guess if that's what you call it, that's what it was.

DOCTOR: You've taken quite a beating all these years . . .

(Once more, I am affirmative in my attitude about her as the victim. She has come into treatment in order to forget a history of victimization and, as treatment unfolds, it becomes my task to help her acknowledge that she is right.)

We then learn that she has this same kind of frightened feeling whenever she is in contact with her siblings. She feels that they will say something to hurt her feelings. They tend to talk about what each of them has done for mother in the past, and always manage to exclude Mrs. R as having made any contribution in that regard. She does not feel scared or so sensitive to hurt with her own children and their spouses.

DOCTOR: Do you remember getting scared when you were a kid?
MRS. R: I always been scared because I know when I do something Mama come and I know what will happen . . . I be scared . . .
DOCTOR: You were scared that she was going to whip you?
MRS. R: I knew I was going to get that whipping.
DOCTOR: But there's nobody around to whip you now . . . why are you still scared?
MRS. R: I don't know . . . but I'd sure like to know.
DOCTOR: I'll tell you . . . you were scared and still are scared when you're around with them because they hurt you so much you'd like to beat the hell out of them.
MRS. R: I guess I would . . . (begins to cry).

(That she is scared even to this day means to me that she must also be very angry, since anger must accompany fear. I therefore decide to tell her directly what I think the anger is that lies behind the fear. I am certain that we have been chipping away at the patient's powerful defense of denial on the right track. The certainty began with the patient's recognition and acceptance of the central issue at the start. Whatever else someone with a chronic sense of hurt may feel, anger is likely to be the most troublesome feeling to manage. Because a patient of this kind is often suggestible, however, the possibility might be raised that she is responding to my suggestions about her feelings and wishes rather than feeling them herself. This explanation may be true and should be determined by future meetings, particularly by the kind of transference that will reveal itself as we come to the termination of treatment.)

Because of the Thanksgiving holiday, the eighth meeting comes two weeks after the seventh.

DOCTOR: How are you?
MRS. R: I'm doing pretty good.
DOCTOR: It's been some time since we last met . . .
MRS. R: It sure have.
DOCTOR: Did you miss me?
MRS. R: Well, maybe I did miss the meeting (giggles).
DOCTOR: Are you a little embarrassed to say that?
MRS. R: No . . . reckon I missed . . . I don't know . . . I just missed being here last Thursday.

(Patients often say that they missed coming here, or that they missed the meeting, in order to avoid saying that they missed seeing the therapist. The patient's giggle, a bit of very unusual behavior for her, gives her away.)

She quickly returns to an almost obsessional preoccupation with the never-ending hurt that she endures in conversations with members of her family whenever the talk turns to the various ways in which the brothers and sisters had been helpful to their parents. No reference is ever made

to the patient's helpfulness in transporting the parents when needed or to
the patient's feeling that, of all the siblings, she worked the hardest to
make the farm the modest success that it was. For the first time in our
interviews, she tells, with clear anger, of how little her efforts were recognized, which I take as a signal to explore her anger and her defense
against it.

DOCTOR: Did you ever say to them, how come they don't remember what you
did?
MRS. R: No.
DOCTOR: Why not?
MRS. R: I don't know.
DOCTOR: Remember what we said last time about how you felt about your
brothers and sisters.
MRS. R: Yeah, I do.
DOCTOR: I said something that you would really like to beat the hell out of
them. Do you remember that?
MRS. R: I remember . . . but I don't know what would really happen if I say
anything . . . what would happen to me . . . I'm afraid what would
happen.
(She hints at some fear about what would happen to her if she ever let
herself feel her anger, and I raise the question of loss of control. She can
only say that her siblings would start to argue with her. Feeling that we
must move on to her anger toward mother, I tell her directly that I believe
she is angrier with her mother than with her siblings. This anger is
justified because mother never forgave the patient before she died.)
MRS. R: Maybe I am . . . I guess I feel she should have knowed better . . .
she was older than all of us and she should have knowed better.
DOCTOR: I get the idea from you that your brother and your sisters seem
pretty nice to you now.
MRS. R: They do pretty good . . . but they can't sit thirty minutes unless
they bring up something . . . but my name is never heard.
DOCTOR: I know somebody who left your name out more than any of them
. . . do you know who I mean?
MRS. R: Yeah . . . my mother, I guess . . . I don't think she ever remember
me while she let me have it (begins to cry).
DOCTOR: One of the things that bothers you is that you feel you're not sup-
posed to hate.
MRS. R: That's the way I feel . . . you're not supposed to hate people.
DOCTOR: And it's sinful to hate people?
MRS. R: That's the way I feel.
DOCTOR: But maybe you have to get that hate out of you first.
MRS. R: I wish I'd know how to get it out.
DOCTOR: You've described something that happened to you years ago but for
you it's as though it happened yesterday.
MRS. R: Sometimes I feel that way.
DOCTOR: I know you do because when you and I first met I asked you what it
was that you most wanted help with . . . remember what you said?

MRS. R: No . . . I can't remember.
DOCTOR: You said you wanted to forget some things.
MRS. R: I wish I could.
DOCTOR: One of the big reasons you haven't been able to forget that thing is because of some of the feelings you have about it that you could never allow yourself . . . and one of those feelings is hate . . . you hated your mother for what she did to you.
(Step by step, the aim has been to help the patient begin to feel what it is that she has been warding off all these years.)
MRS. R: I didn't know that I hated that bad (tears) . . . I can hardly believe that I hated that much . . . I guess it could be true. (Now she is crying audibly.)
DOCTOR: Do you say you guess it could be true because I say so, or does it make sense to you?
MRS. R: It do make sense.

Pressed now to say more about mother, she first tells me what a fine woman mother was. She didn't go "chasing around with men," nor did she smoke or drink. However, the patient then recalls in detail all the whippings mother gave her; mother always believed that all the mischief and fighting were provoked by the patient. Her siblings were never whipped.

DOCTOR: How did you feel when she whipped you?
MRS. R: I guess I was hurt.
DOCTOR: I'm sure you were hurt and I'm sure you felt something else beside hurt.
MRS. R: I guess I felt angry . . . she whipped me with a peach tree switch . . . she would get them and plait them together . . . they was long and limber and hurt more.
DOCTOR: Did you ever feel like you'd like to kill her when she switched you?
MRS. R: No, but I remember one time she whupped me I did curse her . . . she whupped me . . . she made me get on my knees (She is crying loudly now.) . . . she made me put my head in the corner and she whupped me . . . I just told her to keep it up and bust my ass because she's getting her satisfaction but she wasn't hurting me.

As we continue with these recollections, she also remembers that the above whipping was the result of a mischievous joke that a cousin told her mother. When she next met the girl, the patient tried to "put a pitchfork through her head."

(Through all of this, the patient is crying as she relates her misery. At times she is unable to talk until she gains control of her tears and long pauses ensue. She displays a rather remarkable defense against any kind of badness when she reveals the nature of the "curse" that she uttered against her mother. We learn that she was more than a match for her siblings when it came to fist fights, and we see that she was also capable of mayhem.)

DOCTOR: You had lots of reasons for hate to build up inside of you . . . did your mother ever say anything nice to you?

MRS. R: I don't know . . . there was so much hate . . .

DOCTOR: You've been carrying this hate around with you all these years . . . most kids when they're whipped like that think to themselves, I wish you were dead . . . whoever was doing the beating.

MRS. R: I never wished that . . . I don't think I ever wished that . . . I can't imagine that

DOCTOR: But when that girl told you she'd only been kidding, you were going to put a pitchfork through her head.

MRS. R: I don't think nobody should kid about something and somebody who tried to beat me to death.

DOCTOR: That's right . . . so where's your mother now?

MRS. R: If it is that when you do wrong you go to hell, then I guess that's where she is. (This is said angrily as she continues to sob.)
(*The session is coming to an end and I feel it advisable to move away from the intensity of the interview and close by referring to the state of her cough, knowing that that is something she can talk about with justified feelings of distress.*)

The ninth session:

MRS. R: I think I'm doing pretty good, although I've been coughing a lot this week and all night.

DOCTOR: You told me once it was like something stuck.

MRS. R: It feel like something in there . . . it tickles in there . . . I don't know what it is . . . feels like I'm swallowing something.

DOCTOR: You mean as though there's something in there?

MRS. R: It feel like it, but the doctor say he can't find nothing wrong there.

DOCTOR: Would you say it felt like a lump in your throat?

MRS. R: That's the way it feels.
(*Since she starts the session with reference to her bad cough, some further effort is made to understand its meaning to her. Something is in her throat that cannot be expelled. Without specifically identifying the unconscious symbolic meaning of the symptom, we can nevertheless understand the symptom as a means of warding off unacceptable feelings. This understanding is substantiated by all our previous work in the treatment.*)

Asked whether she had been having any thoughts about the previous meeting, she remarked that it seems that she cannot remember things the way she should, that her memory seems to be short.

DOCTOR: Do you know how many more meetings you and I have?

MRS. R: I should . . . I lost track . . . I can't remember.

DOCTOR: What would you guess? How many more do we have?

MRS. R: I'd say about two.

DOCTOR: Do you remember the date I said we would be finished on?

MRS. R: I sure don't.

DOCTOR: Your memory isn't too bad . . . actually we have three more after today.

MRS. R: I didn't remember how many more we have but I did thought about this week . . .

(Her complaint that her memory is short provides us with an appropriate opportunity to raise the question of how much time we have left to finish our work. The question of termination, with its meaning of separation and loss, must be made the center of attention no later than the tenth meeting and is often raised in the ninth. In this instance, the opening that she provided was promptly used. Bad as she claims her memory to be, she is almost correct in her guess about the number of meetings left. In many patients, both the termination date and the number of meetings left are repressed. When asked how many are left, patients often respond with one too few or one too many.)

The patient begins to tell me about one of her sons in Georgia who suddenly picked himself up and left for parts unknown. She is upset about it and remarks that "an old lady told me once when you're raising a crowd of boys, there's always one wanting to do something crazy." We return to the subject of termination.

DOCTOR: Do you worry about the fact that we're only going to have three more meetings after today?

MRS. R: No . . . I guess I'll miss them . . . I don't think about it . . . I'm not worried about . . . I guess I'll miss them.

DOCTOR: Maybe that makes you feel a little sad too?

MRS. R: I don't think so.

(This ninth session is marked by more wandering and ambiguity than usual, which can be seen as a further indication that she is, in fact, perturbed about the approaching end. She can acknowledge that she will miss the meetings but characteristically wards off any feelings about termination.)

For a considerable part of the session she moves off into concerns about the property that she owns with her estranged husband and her fear that she will lose it or that her children will get no share in it. She would like to go down to Georgia to look into the matter with the help of one of her children who lives there. She is able to express considerable feeling about her husband.

MRS. R: I saw him one time when he came to my son's house down there.

DOCTOR: How did you feel when he came?

MRS. R: I guess I feel like it's another person walk in the house . . . like a stranger.

DOCTOR: Like a stranger except for the fact that he's really hurt you in this particular way . . . all your work goes for nothing . . . do you get upset when you think what he did to you?

MRS. R: I spent my best life in something I can't live in.

DOCTOR: Does it make sense to you that you might be angry with him for what he did to you?

MRS. R: Maybe . . . I guess so . . . he has it all.

DOCTOR: Do you know why you're crying?

MRS. R: I don't know but I think it's time now for me to stop crying . . .

DOCTOR: I think you're crying because you have been very angry with your husband . . . some people cry when they are angry.

(I am seeking ways to mobilize the patient's feelings. She has reason to feel sad and angry, but her vigorous denial continues. I tell her that people cry when they are angry; she is aware that she has done a great deal of crying throughout our meetings.)

She then speaks of an opportunity to visit in Georgia, and it becomes evident that she is afraid to go. It is understandable that her fear would be even greater now as a result of the work done in treatment, which has mobilized so many memories and feelings. She comes up with two excuses for not going: first, that she will be going into the hospital for surgery; and second, that she would be going during Christmas week and would not wish to miss our meeting. I remind her that we would not be meeting during that week anyway and that her surgery has been postponed until after we are through.

DOCTOR: Maybe you're afraid to go to Georgia?

MRS. R: Last two times I went down there I got sick . . . I don't know what it come from . . . I went to the house and got sick both times.

DOCTOR: I think you got sick because of so much hurt and anger about what this man has done.

MRS. R: Could be . . . I was sweeping up the rug in that house and I moved one of the chairs and there was some paper on the chair and I sweeped the paper . . . I got so sick I couldn't hardly stand up . . . I felt sick all over. And the last time I went down there my feet and legs swolled up on me . . . I can't see what it come from or nothing but I don't see why it should do it when I'm down there . . . it didn't do that no other place I been.

DOCTOR: What do you think when I say that it seems to me that what makes you sick down there is because you're so angry with him for what he did to you?

MRS. R: I don't know really what to think.

(Now we learn more about the strange conversion symptoms that she suffered in Georgia and why she would hesitate to go back there. I take her side again in pointing out to her the understandably strong feelings she has toward her husband for cheating her out of her house and all the work she has put into it. I go further and identify the feeling that I believe she wards off with the symptoms of the strange sickness she suffered on two previous visits there.)

DOCTOR: You're afraid to go, aren't you?

MRS. R: I don't know . . . I don't know the way I am if I can go to my son's house . . .

DOCTOR: You don't like this subject, do you?

MRS. R: It's the truth, though.

DOCTOR: I mean you don't like for us to talk about it.

MRS. R: I don't mind it.

DOCTOR: Is it upsetting for you?

MRS. R: I guess it should have been talked about.

DOCTOR: Well, we still can . . . next week.

In the tenth session, she informs me that she is leaving for Georgia that very evening in order to try to straighten out the property questions that so much concern her. She says that she is not scared and, in fact, she sounds quite self-assured. There is a long pause. When I inquire what is going on in her mind, she says that she knows now that she has been very angry for a long time and never knew it.

DOCTOR: He hasn't treated you very nicely, has he?

MRS. R: No . . . it went a lot deeper than I thought it did . . . I keep thinking a lot about the time when he left the house . . . I didn't realize it went that deep . . .

DOCTOR: When he abandoned you and you were in such a terrible spot there . . .

MRS. R: I sure was . . . when the people in the war say "under fire"—I think I was under fire at the time.

(Once I identified the feeling for her, she was able to recognize it. Next, it was important to support her and to clarify the nature of her feeling.)

She admits now that she is frightened about the trip, and she recalls the two instances when she became strangely ill.

DOCTOR: Do you have any idea what would do it to you?

MRS. R: I don't know . . . I never believed in them things . . . people say people can do to you and things like that.

DOCTOR: Who's doing it to you?

MRS. R: I don't know who's doing it . . . a lady told me that it happened to her . . . she had to go and leave her house . . . I said that's no good . . . no good to have you working and giving it to somebody else . . . she's sitting there talking and not try to do nothing to help herself . . . so I said I don't want nothing like that and I don't want to bother with nothing like that . . . I know I get off the bus that evening and leave . . . I don't remember what happened . . . I know that I get down near the house, something happened to me every time I go there . . . maybe it's something in my mind . . . my legs swelling up like that . . .

DOCTOR: When you go down there . . . you don't realize it . . . but in your head, in your mind, you have not been able to forget what happened . . . how badly you were treated . . . and you walk into that house down there . . . somewhere in your mind you're remembering all this and how angry you were . . . and how angry you are.

MRS. R: Could be true.

(She has hinted broadly at the possibility of strange spells that people may be able to cast, spells that could cause all kinds of disasters. Yet she has her doubts about such events. The superstition serves the interests of her denial

of her feelings. Once more, I describe the feeling that troubles her, and I add that what goes on in the mind may influence what goes on in the body.)

She says that she never realized how much she was affected by her husband's abandonment of her during the shooting incident. She would never do that to her children, and she adds, "I think we all should have gone down together." She felt sad to think that a father would run off and leave his children under fire.

MRS. R: I just wondered about how he could run off like that and leave me.
DOCTOR: Well, he did, didn't he?
MRS. R: He really did.
DOCTOR: And you're the one who has done all the suffering.
MRS. R: I think I had my portion of suffering.

She reminds herself again that she is going to Georgia to settle on the property. She is prepared to take nothing for herself so long as her children are assured of their rights to the property. But then she comes back to her fear of entering the house that was once hers. I remind her of my statement explaining what happens to her when she goes into that house. She feels that it might be true that she is angry about what happened. I remark that maybe she would like to put a pitchfork through her husband's head; that she doesn't actually have to do that, but that her anger has been preying on her mind for a long time.

(The task of helping her to allow herself to feel can never be accomplished by a single phrase. In most cases, this kind of undoing of denial must be repeated over and over, with additional evidence each time. The evidence is gained from what the patient is saying at the moment and from what she has already told me; thus I remind her of the pitchfork so that she knows she is capable of anger.)

DOCTOR: Tell me, Mrs. R, have you had any more thoughts about your coming to see me here?
MRS. R: I did thought . . . you said we had three more times . . . and I was wondering whether that was going to be enough or what . . . maybe it will have to do. (She begins to cry.)

(Despite the important ongoing events in her life, it must be kept in mind that we are in the termination phase of the treatment. Having just reminded her of her anger, or at least the possibility that she possesses such a feeling, I switch to the immediate therapeutic situation, which could also produce anger in her. I do not expect her to be able to verbalize that feeling at this point; however, work on the issue of termination must not be neglected.)

She promptly returns to the question of her trip to Georgia. This move serves to clarify in my mind that anger is present in both situations. Her aim is to avoid discussion of termination. Unconsciously, the issue of termination persists. Recognizing this, I stay with her feelings about the coming termination rather than discussing what awaits her in Georgia.

DOCTOR: I think you also had on your mind the fact that after today we have only two more times that you and I will meet . . . I think that bothers you too.

MRS. R: I think so (crying) . . . it was hard for me to get straightened out . . .

DOCTOR: I suppose then I shouldn't let you go . . . I see that it makes you sad . . . maybe it makes you angry too . . .

MRS. R: Maybe . . . I don't want to feel that way . . . I don't want to be angry.

DOCTOR: But you do worry whether that'll be enough for you to get straightened out.

MRS. R: I was thinking about that.

DOCTOR: Do you think you're going to miss me?

MRS. R: I know I will.

DOCTOR: We're going to meet two more times and then I let you go . . . do you think it's something like what happened with your husband . . . you needed him . . . you needed his help . . . and he just beat it . . . do you think it's something of the same?

MRS. R: I don't think it's the same.

DOCTOR: But you feel the need for help.

MRS. R: (Crying.) That's the way I've been feeling . . . I feel like I need more help . . . I feel like something's not all right . . . I can't tell you what it is . . . I just feel that something is not right.

DOCTOR: Something is not right . . . right here . . . between you and me?

MRS. R: That's right.

DOCTOR: We will have time to figure that one out too . . . maybe that's what we should think about most when we meet again . . . that you feel there's something not right about you . . . I hope you have a good trip down there and get the work done.

MRS. R: I hope so.

DOCTOR: And maybe you don't have to be as afraid as you thought you'd be.

MRS. R: I sure hope not.

(Further preparation for the termination is achieved by helping the patient to appreciate that there is something troublesome going on between us. My next comments aim at supporting her in the trip she is about to make.)

Mrs. R arrived promptly for her eleventh meeting and said that she was doing pretty well. Her mission to Georgia had not accomplished much as far as the property was concerned. She had met her husband and felt that they were like strangers. She assured him that her only interest was in "looking for things that I worked for before I leave." A friend suggested that she might have to go to court to get her half of the property, but her own idea was that her children should get together and get her husband to make a will in which they would inherit the land.

DOCTOR: But nothing in it for you?

MRS. R: Nothing in it for me.

DOCTOR: How do you feel about that?

MRS. R: Well, as long as my children get it anyway . . .

DOCTOR: You went to your house there . . . did you stay there?

MRS. R: Yes, I did . . . two nights.

DOCTOR: And how did you feel while you were there?

MRS. R: I didn't feel sick or anything . . . I just felt, I guess, lonely . . .

DOCTOR: Lonely . . . but no swelling up or anything like that?

MRS. R: Not this time.

DOCTOR: You told me that you were somewhat afraid about going down there.

MRS. R: Nothing didn't happen this time . . . so I guess I do feel better about going down there 'cause this time it seemed like nothing bothered me.

DOCTOR: Are you surprised?

MRS. R: I really was surprised 'cause the last two times I went down . . .

DOCTOR: What do you think made the difference?

MRS. R: I don't know . . . no idea . . .

DOCTOR: I think I have an idea why it was different.

MRS. R: I sure would like to hear it (laughs).

DOCTOR: This time, because of our meeting here and talking about all this . . . it was the first time you realized something about your feelings . . . about your mother . . . about your husband . . . you had all those buried inside of you.

(Having learned early in our meeting that she had not had any physical symptoms during her visit, I took advantage of her good feelings about herself in this regard and brought to her attention the fact that her lack of symptoms was a direct result of our work in previous sessions.)

She continues with further details of her meeting with her husband and his apparent refusal to grant her any property rights. She feels that he is an angry and confused man and that something is not right with him. She denies having any negative feelings toward him, although she agrees with me when I say that she must feel cheated by him of what is rightfully hers.

DOCTOR: How do you feel about him?

MRS. R: I don't have no feelings . . . only I know he's not doing the right thing.

DOCTOR: You don't have any feelings about him: I don't know about that . . . you mean you don't mind what he's done?

MRS. R: I mind what he's done.

DOCTOR: Then you do have some feelings about it.

MRS. R: I don't know what it can be.

DOCTOR: You have tears in your eyes . . . what kind of feeling is that?

MRS. R: I guess he's stingy . . . trying to take everything I worked for.

DOCTOR: Yes . . . and what kind of feeling does it give you?

MRS. R: Terrible feelings . . .

DOCTOR: Sad?

MRS. R: Yes.

DOCTOR: Perhaps you have some angry thoughts about him?

MRS. R: Probably (crying) . . . I don't know but it hurts . . . I don't know what I can do about it.

DOCTOR: You know that you feel hurt about . . . you feel hurt . . . at this point I guess you don't know what you can do about the property . . . but you know how you feel.

MRS. R: That's right . . . yes, I do.

DOCTOR: And it's not very good, is it?

MRS. R: No . . . it's not.

(I take every opportunity to continue the repetitive work of helping her to undo her denial and identify her own feelings. She is able to say that "it hurts." Since this patient has previously used denial and somatization extensively to ward off feelings, her awareness of hurt is a significant sign of progress.)

I inquire about her thoughts since returning to Boston and she says that she thought about coming to see me today. She did not know what she was going to say since she felt she had not accomplished her mission. I wondered if she felt somewhat ashamed to have to tell me that, and she acknowledged that that was the case. I told her that I thought she had done very well considering how frightened she had been about going there in the first place. She repeated that she had been troubled with the feeling that she had failed me and herself as well.

(I was very much pleased that she had been able to make her visit without developing any symptoms. From her point of view, however, she had been a failure; she had not been able to clear up the matter of her property rights. Moreover, she felt that she had failed me. This feeling could be understood as partly arising from her need to please, to be thought well of, and as partly very much related to the fact that treatment was coming to an end. If she had failed me, that might be sufficient reason for me to get rid of her. I would not expect her to consider this possibility consciously.)

I then asked her if she remembered anything that she and I had talked about the last time we met. She denied any recollection.

DOCTOR: Do you remember us talking about how much more time we had?

MRS. R: Yes, I do.

DOCTOR: Have you thought about that?

MRS. R: I sure did.

DOCTOR: When were you thinking about that?

MRS. R: All along . . .

DOCTOR: Did you think about it today?

MRS. R: I sure did . . . after all this I don't know if I could . . . didn't know what was going to happen.

DOCTOR: Will you explain that to me more?

MRS. R: I just feel like I wasn't ready to give this up right now. (She begins to cry.) . . . I think I need to go and get this operation and have it over with . . . if I could do that . . . come back, or what I could do . . .

DOCTOR: Come back where?

MRS. R: Here.

DOCTOR: You mean to see me?

MRS. R: That's right.

(She is deeply concerned about the impending termination and separation and hints strongly about a course of action—namely, that she will have her surgery as a means of postponing the inevitable end.)

DOCTOR: You don't like the idea of us stopping after next week?

MRS. R: I don't feel that way.

DOCTOR: Why do you think we'll be stopping?

MRS. R: I don't know.

DOCTOR: Do you know what your feelings are about us stopping?

MRS. R: Not really . . . I just don't feel right about it . . . I just have these bad feelings . . . it hurts . . . (cries audibly).

DOCTOR: You feel hurt . . . who is it that is hurting you . . . who is hurting you, Mrs. R?

MRS. R: The kid's father is hurting me . . . I guess it's my sisters and brothers and everybody . . .

DOCTOR: Anybody else?

MRS. R: My mother too, I guess . . .

DOCTOR: I don't think that's the whole thing . . . I think you feel that I'm hurting you, too.

MRS. R: I don't feel like that.

DOCTOR: Well, whose idea was it, yours or mine, that next week would be the last meeting?

MRS. R: You're the one said that next week would be the last meeting.

DOCTOR: You wouldn't say it's the last meeting if it was up to you, would you?

MRS. R: I hope not.

DOCTOR: Because if it was up to you we would keep on meeting . . .

MRS. R: We sure would.

DOCTOR: So I must be hurting you too.

MRS. R: I couldn't really say that.

DOCTOR: I think you're afraid to say that . . . I think you have the feeling that I'm kind of deserting you under fire.

MRS. R: No, I couldn't say that . . . because the way you feel after all this long time I should have felt better than the way I do . . . I could never say that you're deserting me . . .

DOCTOR: So it's all your fault? . . . you don't think I'm deserting you under fire the way your husband did, but you're saying that you should be much better than you are, so you must feel that you have disappointed me.

MRS. R: I've had so many disappointments.

DOCTOR: Yes, but remember now . . . you're not disappointing me . . . I'm disappointing you.

MRS. R: I guess I have to pray harder.

DOCTOR: You know why we're stopping next week . . . because I think you've learned enough about yourself and what's happened to you . . . that you can manage better and that you can get along without me.

MRS. R: I don't know, but I'll try.

DOCTOR: I want you to know that we're not stopping because of anything bad that you did . . . and we're not stopping because I think you failed to accomplish what you set out to do in Georgia . . . and we're not stopping because I think you're bad. Do you hear me?

MRS. R: Yes, I do.

DOCTOR: The thing is that you don't want me to leave you.

MRS. R: Not altogether, I don't think . . . just maybe if I feel the need I could come back some time.

DOCTOR: Maybe you won't feel the need . . . maybe you're going to do much better than you think.

MRS. R: I hope so.

DOCTOR: You know something about yourself for the first time . . . how angry you have been at your mother, at your husband, and some other people for the bad way they treated you.

MRS. R: I really didn't know that I felt that bad towards them.

DOCTOR: You have a right to feel that way.

MRS. R: It's a terrible load to carry.

DOCTOR: What is?

MRS. R: Hate.

DOCTOR: I think you're going to be rid of that load . . . you've always carried it kind of hiding inside you . . . and now I think you can be rid of it.

MRS. R: I hope so.

DOCTOR: Shall we talk more about it next week? About that hate that you had buried . . . sort of hiding inside of you all these years . . . that's been hurting you . . .

MRS. R: That's right . . . I really would like to talk about that.

(She has not been able to tolerate her "load of hate," and with it, her deep sense of being bad and unacceptable. As we come to the final meeting, it would be impossible for her not to reexperience the very conflict that brought her to treatment via the long detour through the medical clinic. We have probed the factual roots and, even more important, the affective roots of her chronic pain.)

Shortly before the appointed time for the twelfth session, I was informed that Mrs. R had gone to the hospital outpatient department at 3 P.M.—exactly twenty-four hours before our meeting time—complaining of right upper quadrant pain. She had been admitted to the hospital, presumably for gall bladder surgery. She had asked a nurse to call the psychiatry department and leave me the message that she would not be in today. The message was received by one of the psychiatric residents participating in our seminar, who promptly visited Mrs. R to convince her to come to this last session. Mrs. R refused to come.

I assumed that Mrs. R sought to avoid our separation and had unconsciously chosen a somatic avoidance mode. At my urging, the resident made a second visit to her and this time succeeded in gaining her agreement to come. My certainty about the relation of her belly pain to separation was fortified by her expectation that, if her situation had been at all acute, she would not have been permitted to walk over to another building for our meeting. Moreover, it will be recalled that in the previous meeting she had already hinted at her need for surgery in the midst of our talking about the end of treatment.

There is another point to be made. A sound understanding of basic psychoanalytic theory and concepts as the psychodynamic basis of any kind of psychotherapy allows the therapist to make certain assumptions with confidence. The fact that the patient's abdominal pain occurred exactly one day before our last meeting, and that her arrival at the OPD was exactly twenty-four hours before our meeting time, was her way of delivering a clearly understandable, albeit wholly unconscious, message. In the light of the total therapeutic situation, I chose not to make an issue of her entering the hospital as an avoidance. Instead, I decided to accept the reality of her new pain and to work instead with the pain of the central issue.

Mrs. R appeared wearing a robe over a hospital gown; she gave no evidence of acute pain. She said she had pain in her belly and her back, as well as a headache. She had not yet been given any medication in the hospital. She expects to undergo surgery but has not been told when it will take place. She hopes something will be done for her various pains.

DOCTOR: Did you have any feelings about the fact that this was going to be our last meeting?

MRS. R: Yes, I did.

DOCTOR: Let's talk about that.

MRS. R: I just keep going over in my mind this is the last day . . .

DOCTOR: When you say this is the last day, you sound very sad.

MRS. R: I guess I feel . . . still feel that I need to talk more.

DOCTOR: You are saying you feel there is a need to talk more, and what am I saying?

MRS. R: I don't know.

DOCTOR: Oh yes you do . . . I've been saying that I think you are going to manage all right.

MRS. R: That's right, too . . . and I'm hoping I can . . .

DOCTOR: If I said that I think you also feel angry toward me, would that make sense to you?

MRS. R: It wouldn't . . . I don't feel that . . . feeling angry at you . . . I don't see how I could . . .

DOCTOR: Suppose I said that you feel hurt?

MRS. R: I don't know . . . I know I'm not feeling angry.

DOCTOR: You know you're not feeling angry at me but not so sure whether you feel hurt or don't feel hurt.

MRS. R: That's true.
(The work of identifying her feelings for her is unceasing. The one feeling she is most able to recognize is her hurt.)

DOCTOR: I think it would be natural for you to feel hurt . . . because you would feel that I don't care about you . . . if I cared about you I'd say O.K., let's talk some more . . . remember, Mrs. R, that's what brought you here . . . you felt that you had tried so hard, worked so hard in your life, and that you were lonely and hurt.

MRS. R: That's right (very affirmatively).

DOCTOR: Your mother hurt you . . . your husband hurt you . . . some others in your family hurt you, and I guess you felt that they couldn't have loved you very much if they did that to you . . . and it would be natural for you to feel hurt and feel that if I say that this is all we're going to meet, then wouldn't it be natural for you to feel that maybe I don't care much about you either?

MRS. R: I don't think I could feel that ways . . . I know all doctors have their limit, I guess . . . I mean they have other patients.

DOCTOR: And someone else is more important?

MRS. R: Oh no, I didn't say that either.

DOCTOR: Aren't you important enough to be seen more?

MRS. R: I hope so.

(In this last session, the main aim will be to elaborate and clarify the feelings that will arise as the result of termination and separation. The degree to which I actively interpose my remarks in the final session depends on the patient. For example, a patient who is more verbal and in closer contact with her feelings will require somewhat less intervention. Every effort must be made to clarify the central issue in terms of both the past events that gave rise to it and the affective situation of separation that the patient is now experiencing. The patient's affective response to the separation cannot be very different from the chronic pain that led to the need for help. From the moment that a patient develops a positive relationship to the therapist, rivalry with the therapist's other patients is always present. The patient is invariably saddened by the knowledge that he is only a patient and that the therapist is just doing his job. The patient then feels that there must be some other or others who are more important to the therapist. Mrs. R denies this feeling, but the way she spoke of every doctor having his limits clearly suggested not only that I had had enough of her and had done all I could for her, but also that there were more important others for me to attend to.)

We discuss her various ongoing problems and my belief that she will be able to manage them. I continue to raise questions about what she is feeling; I emphasize the hurt and how much it justifies the anger that she has hidden so deeply inside her. I remind her that one day she may come to feel that I too hurt her by letting her go, and that she might then feel angry at me. She does not think this can happen.

DOCTOR: How do you feel about me?

MRS. R: I feel that you helped me a whole lot to understand myself a little better . . . a whole lot better.

DOCTOR: Do you love me?

(This may sound painfully presumptuous, but it was said for three reasons: first, she has claimed to have only feelings of love for people; second, I am aware of her positive feelings for me; and third, if she can speak of her positive feelings, her feelings of hurt about separation may become more available and apparent.)

MRS. R: I think I love pretty much everybody . . . I hope I do.

DOCTOR: You loved your mother and she hurt you . . . there was a time that you loved your husband and he hurt you . . . and while you may disagree with me, I hurt you too because you said you would like to talk more . . . but there is a big difference . . . I'm not seeing you more not because I don't want you or don't like you and want to get rid of you . . . that's not it at all . . . I'm not going to see you further because I think you can manage it by yourself.

MRS. R: I'll do what I can . . . and I'll try awful hard.

To relieve the intensity of the moment, I shift to the reality of her present life circumstances and inquire about her activities at home, at church, and with friends. This topic winds down and she becomes silent. A long pause follows.

DOCTOR: Is this very painful for you . . . this saying good-bye . . . you and me . . .

MRS. R: (Sighs.) I guess there's no need for it to be painful . . . there's no need to really take it to heart . . .

DOCTOR: It really is not easy to say good-bye, is it?

MRS. R: I guess not.

DOCTOR: But remember, I'm not saying good-bye to you because I want to be rid of you . . . I think we've accomplished what needed to be done . . . you've been hurt . . . and with good cause you've been angry, but you haven't allowed yourself to know that . . . and those angry feelings have made you feel sick, sad, and depressed . . . and hurting all over.

MRS. R: They really did and I never did know it. (She is crying.)

DOCTOR: Is there anything you'd like to say to me before we say good-bye?

MRS. R: I have enjoyed being here . . . talking with you . . . things you let me know that I didn't know . . . to straighten my mind up.

DOCTOR: I want you to know that I've enjoyed talking with you . . . and with what you know now, I think you can feel better and be easier on yourself.

MRS. R: I think I can . . . I'll try hard.

DOCTOR: Good-bye, Sophie.

MRS. R: Thank you.

(As we say good-bye, I call her by her first name for the first time. This was not planned; it was spontaneous and felt right. In retrospect, I could understand that its purpose was to express a closeness born out of sharing a significant experience with the patient. This is in contrast to the tendency of many therapists to think that they are diminishing the distance between themselves and their patients by immediately calling patients by their first names.)

Follow-up session ten months later

The immediate difference I noted was Mrs. R's animation. The depressed, hopeless feeling that was so pervasive through most of the treatment was gone. She was alert, cheerful, and responsive. She quickly told of her enormous relief at getting rid of her chronic cough. The cough stopped shortly after treatment ended.

Nothing had changed in respect to the property in Georgia. Asked if she still talked about the shooting incident with her brother years before, she remarked that she had spoken to her sister about it recently. She added that she feels she will never forget what happened, but she is now able to forgive those involved in the incident. She felt that this was an effective solution, and I concurred. Interestingly, when I asked her if she recalled what problem she and I initially agreed to work on, she said, "Hating my mother . . . that's what it was . . . I know it was true, too, 'cause I know I feel a lot better . . . I didn't think a person could get so sick from that and then get a lot better."

I inquired about the state of her gall bladder. "I stayed in there about two weeks but they didn't find anything . . . it [the pain] disappeared somewhere . . . I'm sure glad it disappeared . . . [laughs] . . . I didn't want to be cut . . ."

She is getting along well with all the members of her family except for the brother who once tried to kill her; he lives in New York and she has no wish to see him. She makes quilts, has sold some, and is considering a housework job. Asked if she had any thoughts about me, she replied, "I thought about you right often . . . I felt very good about you because I know you done a wonderful thing for me . . . overcome all that chokin' and everything else . . . I was dying by degrees . . . it's gone."

Throughout the interview, she did not hesitate to look at me directly. When I thanked her for coming in, she said, "I think this talk will help me a lot, too."

The central issue had effectively reached the painful feeling of anger that she had vigorously warded off with somatic complaints and depression. At the time of this writing, more than two years after the follow-up interview, I called her and learned that she continues to do well and is without symptoms.

10

Perspective

We have attempted to serve two purposes. First, we have tried to specify conceptually the place of time-limited psychotherapy in the theoretical framework of the psychoanalytic therapies. We have attempted to demonstrate that major symptomatic—and even characterological—change can occur by the proper utilization of an interplay between time and the central issue. We have not attempted to present time-limited psychotherapy as a "miracle cure" or as a competitor with other therapies. We do contend, however, that it is an extremely powerful mode of treatment, has sound theoretical underpinnings, and differs from all other forms of analytic psychotherapy.

Our second goal in preparing this volume was to present case material that covered a relatively broad spectrum of psychopathology. While we have not covered all the diagnostic categories that would benefit from time-limited psychotherapy, we have tried to illustrate how time-limited psychotherapy is chosen as a treatment modality, how a central issue is determined, and how time-limited psychotherapy is conducted. In this we have also tried to confirm our theoretical notions.

Our aims in this book have been relatively modest. We have not attempted controlled studies, nor have we developed numerical guidelines for case selection. We simply do not believe that at this point the information we have gathered lends itself to such precision. In the future, however, controlled outcome studies will certainly be important. And, of course, more precise criteria for case selection will need to be developed when the data warrant them. Finally, further refinement of the technique of time-limited psychotherapy will be another of our future research tasks.

Time-limited psychotherapy is as rewarding as it is difficult. It imposes its own kind of discipline on the therapist, who must always pay close attention to the unfolding therapeutic process. Time-limited psychotherapy begins with the formulation of the central issue, based on the data obtained in the evaluation interviews. The presentation of the central issue to the patient must be carefully organized. From the moment the details of the treatment proposal are accepted, the central issue becomes the therapist's guidepost for understanding both the process and the transference, including the all-important termination phase.

The therapist must always be alert to diversions by the patient; i.e., material that is clearly unrelated to the central issue and therefore resistant or inhibitory to the task at hand. The rapid accumulation of patient data demands that the therapist quickly grasp their meaning as well as their implications for the therapeutic situation. In short, the therapist must keep well ahead of the patient. While this dictum may be taken as a given in all psychotherapies, it assumes special importance in time-limited psychotherapy, which does not allow for future opportunities to rectify any "missed" understandings. Similarly, a tired or distracted therapist cannot coast with the feeling that there will always be time to get back to work. The time limit effectively precludes therapist passivity just as it precludes patient passivity. Interventions by the therapist—to gain significant historical information, to make clarifications and interpretations—call for active engagement with the patient. Most important to the therapist's posture and activity is a sound understanding, reinforced by good clinical experience with the long-term treatment of patients, of the unconscious functions of defense, of transference, of associations that may seem meaningless to the patient, and of affects that may be disguised in many different ways.

The rewards for the patient, of course, lie in the extent to which he feels he has been helped. The therapist, too, shares in that kind of reward. The therapist will find that, even in cases where treatment goals were not fully attained, patients have learned much about themselves. The context and content of that learning can only be helpful, since it is never devastating to the patient's defensive needs. We have not yet seen a patient who was injured in any way by time-limited psychotherapy, the outcome notwithstanding. In addition, all of our patients have gained a better understanding of the genesis and nature of their distorted self-image. The acceptance of the central issue, as we have constructed it, is rarely followed by anything less than the completion of treatment. A major exception is the kind of hysterical character we discussed in Chapter 4. Time-limited psychotherapy is a fascinating mode of treatment that rapidly becomes an intensive experience for both patient and therapist. This level of intensity remains throughout the twelve sessions. Even the weary therapist in a late Friday afternoon session will find little difficulty in staying alert, awake, and actively engaged.

We do not believe that it is appropriate to compare the goals and results of time-limited psychotherapy—or any mode of brief psychotherapy—with those of long-term psychotherapy or psychoanalysis. The choice of treatment modality will depend on the needs of a given patient at a particular time. There are patients for whom any kind of brief psychotherapy is contraindicated. Certain patients require regular visits for many years in order to remain socially viable. In all cases, we must give consideration to the patient's own goals. Thus, those patients who want the treatment that will provide the greatest degree of self-knowledge and offer the greatest possibility for personality reorganization choose psychoanalysis. Psychoanalysis is the only treatment that can probe the most defended-against and conflicted wishes, fears, and fantasies. In some cases, the treatment modality may need to be changed as a result of events that have occurred during therapy.

There are vast numbers of people in emotional pain for whom a brief form of psychotherapy is indicated. Most patients are interested in whatever treatment will provide the greatest relief as quickly as possible. Ideally, the economic factor should not enter into one's decision about treatment modality, but the reality in this country demands that we consider it. The availability of low-cost or free long-term treatment in institutions and agencies is rapidly diminishing as third-party payments become more universal. Low-cost psychoanalysis is available only in cities with psychoanalytic training institutes. Time-limited psychotherapy and other forms of brief psychotherapy allow for the treatment of many more patients in a short time. Treatment goals are limited, and the patient expects to achieve some degree of relief reasonably quickly.

Something more must be said in respect to the therapist who automatically prefers an open-ended treatment arrangement, even in so-called "brief" psychotherapy. Such a preference sacrifices the conscious and unconscious meaning of time and its influence on the treatment process. As a result, guidelines that illuminate the process are lost when the element of time and our particular kind of central issue are not given their full weight. Any form of brief psychotherapy must have an endpoint; to the extent that the end remains uncertain and obscure, the patient and therapist may fail to do the important work of termination and separation. One may question whether it suffices to arrange termination with a patient, say, three or four weeks beforehand. In both psychoanalysis and long-term psychotherapy, the termination date is usually agreed on *at least* four to six months in advance. The reason is that, as repeated clinical experience has shown, the agreement to end treatment results in the rapid mobilization of the patient's defenses to forestall termination and the accompanying distress of separation and loss. Too often, the patient in long-term treatment seeks to separate from the therapist in the same way that he separated from the important earlier persons in his life—with all the old ambivalences intact. It is our position that, regardless of the number of sessions, there is a distinct advantage in setting the end date of treatment at the start of any short-term psychotherapy.

The question may be raised whether the above considerations hold true for brief treatment procedures that consist of as few as six sessions. Such procedures are often used for crisis intervention, in which the treatment goal is simply to bring order to an immediate, difficult life circumstance. The opportunity for abreaction—along with guidance, counseling, and mobilization of external resources—usually suffices in these cases.

There are additional aspects of time-limited psychotherapy that warrant consideration. Some patients have read *Time Limited Psychotherapy* or have heard the authors lecture and demonstrate the process. Familiarity with our clearly delineated therapeutic model leads certain patients to look for the expected reactions in themselves—that is, the abreaction of the first phase, with its positive transference and alliance; the ambivalence of the second phase; and the reactions to termination of the third phase. This kind of attention by the patient is a particular kind of resistance that the ambiguity of other modes of psychotherapy avoids. It is a resistance against experiencing feelings and can be managed in the light of the central issue. Coping devices, which have served to keep out of awareness feelings of being controlled by others, of being a loser, of being helpless, inadequate, cheated, unrewarded, inferior, or unwanted, are also concealing powerful affects that all patients will seek to avoid. The informed patient will follow the book, so to speak, and will comply as a means of avoiding the strong feelings and the fear of retaliation. Such resistance rapidly becomes a transference issue within the meaning of the central issue; the therapist must deal with it directly, albeit gently and with understanding. The release of feelings by the patient effectively undoes this particular kind of resistance.

We are very much aware of the problems of patient selection. For the most part, clinicians must make their own judgments about the suitability of a particular therapy on the basis of the data they have accumulated about the nature of the patient's problems. Obviously, the greater the therapist's experience, the sooner and more confidently will an appropriate choice be made. On the other hand, every experienced clinician knows that the trial of therapy may reveal a gross diagnostic error calling for a change in the treatment modality.

In our chapter on the selection of patients, we discussed some specific indications for time-limited psychotherapy. We also made the more general observation that, despite evidence of serious early difficulties, in assessing the patient's present capacity to function, the overall state of the patient's ego strength may be a more accurate indicator of the suitability of time-limited psychotherapy. Here again, the major desideratum hinges on the clinician's judgment, which is of course subject to error. Our tendency is to expand the variety of patients for whom time-limited psychotherapy is indicated since, if a serious diagnostic error has been made, a change in treatment can be effected smoothly and usefully. In this connection, it is highly unusual for the therapist not to have a secure diagnostic understanding of the patient after the first two to four sessions. The search for more refined selection procedures continues.

If we may venture another generalization, it would be that experienced clinicians tend to be more resistant to the idea of time-limited psychotherapy than are the less experienced. Experienced clinicians tend to be comfortable with certain modes of therapy and to become uneasy, even anxious, about the prospect of trying something new. Opposition to brief psychotherapy per se is no longer of any consequence; most clinicians practice some kind of brief treatment. The definition of brief treatment, however, varies with each practitioner.

Time-limited psychotherapy, in contrast, has already been defined. Thus, any resistance to using this modality must relate to specific, serious objections. We believe that the major objection is to setting an end date at the start of therapy, although it is rarely stated in such direct terms. Instead, objections are made to the therapist-patient relationship suggested by our model. For example, some object that there is no room for the patient to decide how much treatment he needs; he is forced to accept twelve sessions. We have made the point that the patient is offered the opportunity to accept or reject the treatment plan. Our kind of central issue rings so true for the patient that rejection is unusual. A few patients do reject the treatment proposal, either as a result of their particular personality organization (diagnosis) or because they seek a more intensive examination of their personality (i.e., long-term psychotherapy or psychoanalysis). A final rejection by the patient is honored, and some other kind of therapy is agreed on.

A final important consideration is that, in comparison to other psychotherapies, time-limited psychotherapy can be taught to therapists with less interference from their idiosyncracies or personality problems than is found in the teaching and practice of other psychotherapies. We have already said that time-limited psychotherapy is not easy, is not for the inexperienced, and should follow on enough experience with long-term psychotherapy. All varieties of psychotherapy are difficult and require intensive training, careful supervision, and firm self-discipline. We believe that all therapists should have a personal analysis, or at least exposure to personal long-term psychotherapy, as part of their commitment to becoming the best possible therapist.

Our model of time-limited psychotherapy, with its particular kind of central issue and unique use of time, offers a framework and a set of guidelines unlike those of any other brief psychotherapy. The experience gained in practicing it fleshes out the readily grasped framework. The psychodynamic concepts that all therapists study—and that many have difficulty with in practice—become graphically and affectively visible in time-limited psychotherapy. Our experience in teaching this model to psychiatric residents confirms its educational value in enhancing the resident's understanding of the dynamic processes in patients. Ida Mann's experience in conducting seminars for social workers in the theory and practice of time-limited psychotherapy has further validated our position that this treatment method addresses the needs of therapists with unusual clarity.

Index

Commentary

"Dr. James Mann and his associates at Boston University Medical School are among the most talented of a growing number of psychoanalytically oriented short-term therapists. Their unique innovation is not only to keep psychotherapy brief, but to limit it to twelve sessions.

"What impresses the reader most about Mann and Goldman is not their theorizing but their deftness as clinicians. The sessions are sometimes summarized and sometimes verbatim transcripts. A wide variety of psychopathology is represented: an acute phobic reaction, a severe hypochondriacal reaction, two hysterical character neuroses, and a hysterical conversion. The authors concentrate on the inner life of the patient and can treat people despite lack of verbal fluency due to racial, religious, and socioeconomic reasons.

"[Deciding] when short-term or when long-term therapy is indicated is the salient task for psychodynamic therapists in the years ahead. Drs. Mann and Goldman have substantially contributed to this task."

—Ronald J. Karpf, Ph.D.
American Journal of Psychotherapy